>–•–•–O–•–•–< The Other >–•–•–O–•–•–<
Jerome K. Jerome

The Other Jerome K. Jerome

Selected & Introduced by Martin Green

First published in this form 1984
This edition published 2009

The History Press
The Mill, Brimscombe Port
Stroud, Gloucestershire, GL5 2QG
www.thehistorypress.co.uk

Introduction & selection © Martin Green, 1984, 2009

British Library Cataloguing in Publication Data.
A catalogue record for this book is available from the British Library.

ISBN 978 1 84588 635 6

Printed in Great Britain

Contents

Introduction   7

Birth and Parentage   12
My Life and Times (1926)

I Became an Actor   24
On the Stage—and Off (1885)

My Last Appearance   31
On the Stage—and Off (1885)

Silhouettes   35
The Idler (1892)

Variety Patter   43
The Idler (1892)

The Servant Girl   51
Stage-Land (1889)

The Woman of the Saeter   55
The Idler (1893)

The Ghost of the Marchioness of Appleford   66
The Observations of Henry and Others (1901)

The Passing of the Third Floor Back   77
The Passing of the Third Floor Back (1907)

Diary of a Pilgrimage   95
Diary of a Pilgrimage (1891)

The Street of the Blank Wall   104
Malvina of Brittany (1916)

His Evening Out   123
Malvina of Brittany (1916)

The War   142
My Life and Times (1926)

Introduction

This selection from the works of Jerome K. Jerome is an attempt to show that the popular conception of him as simply a writer of a couple of very funny books does him an injustice. It is also hoped that it will encourage his admirers to read further into Jerome and to establish him as a popular author in his own right. Jerome's output was not particularly prodigious by the standards of the time when compared with his contemporaries such as H. G. Wells, Rudyard Kipling or Rider Haggard, but in fact for a number of years he was not only writing on his own behalf, but also editing *The Idler*, a monthly magazine which he had co-founded with two others in 1892, and also *To-Day*, a popular weekly paper which ran from 1893 to 1905. His association with both these periodicals ended in 1898, as the result of a disastrous libel action—for all parties except the lawyers, that is—in which the plaintiff, a company promoter from Leeds, was awarded a farthing damages against the editor of *To-Day*. As no order was made as to costs, both parties had to pay their own, Jerome's being £9000 and those of Samson Fox, the plaintiff, being £11,000 (in today's terms these sums would be breathtaking). Both parties shook hands after the case and Samson Fox said he was returning to Leeds to strangle his solicitors and he hoped Jerome would do the same. Jerome only managed to salve his financial fortunes by the sale of his interest in both papers.

During the period leading up to the libel case Jerome had been putting in a fourteen-hour day and was still able to find time to write for the theatre as well as for a nationwide lecture tour.

Jerome's career as a writer developed from unpromising beginnings—unless, that is, you believe that poverty is the nursemaid of genius. Jerome Klapka Jerome was born in Walsall, Staffordshire, in 1859, the second son and fourth child of a mine-owning Nonconformist preacher whose fortunes collapsed almost immediately after his son's arrival in the world; the Jerome pit was flooded on the day that Jerome junior achieved his first birthday. The dowry that Jerome's mother had brought to her husband (her father had been a prosperous Swansea solicitor) had been sunk into the pit, after an attempt at farming and stone-quarrying in Devon. With what little there was left, Jerome's father came up to London and tried his hand in the ironmongery trade in the East End, sending for his family when Jerome was three years old. Jerome's earliest memories were of the grim poverty of the surrounding streets, and he was extremely lucky to get a place at the St Marylebone Grammar School, to which he travelled every day from Poplar. He remained there until he was fourteen, shortly after the death of his father and just before that of his mother. He then entered the bleakest period of his life, living alone and working as a clerk for the Great Western Railway at Euston. He broke away from his clerical existence by taking a job as a schoolmaster in Clapham and then, screwing his courage to the sticking point, taking to the stage. It was his experience as an actor touring the country that gave him his first success as a writer, when a series of comic sketches he wrote about the stage were published in a popular paper and then subsequently published as a book, *On the Stage—and Off*. From his beginning as an itinerant journalist covering coroners' and police courts, his career as a writer proceeded with remarkable speed.

Jerome became a popular author, and a playwright whose plays ran successfully in London and New York, though he never managed to get away from the slur of vulgarity that *Punch* attached to him when it dubbed him 'Arry K. 'Arry.

In the year he wrote his most famous book, *Three Men in a Boat*, he married one Georgina Stanley who already had a daughter of her own. She had another daughter by Jerome and by all accounts they lived happily together thereafter.

He had grown fond of Germany and the Germans after residing in Dresden, and though he initially welcomed the First World War he was unable to believe the atrocity stories put about, and he said so publicly. He was sent by the British Government with a delegation to America to enlist sympathy for the British cause and on his return his sense of impotence and frustration led him to try to enlist, but he was told he was too old. However, he managed to join a French ambulance unit serving on the Western Front.

His only work of importance after the war was his *My Life and Times* published in 1926, much more attractively written than the fey and sentimental attempts at autobiographical fiction which he produced in *Paul Kelver*, a novel greeted with tepid enthusiasm by the reviewers and which he thought was his greatest work. He fell ill while on a motoring trip to England in 1927 and died in Northampton, not a congenial place for writers, as John Clare had discovered earlier.

The selection that makes up this collection gives a portrait of Jerome K. Jerome in his own words that complements his own memoirs and reflects his interests and achievements. Beginning and ending with chapters from *My Life and Times*, it encapsulates his experience as an actor while giving examples of his occasional pieces from *The Idler*, as well as a number of his short stories.

While Jerome was always in danger of veering towards a kind of mystical sentimentality (demonstrated deliberately here by the inclusion of 'The Passing of the Third Floor Back', a short story which, turned into a play, assured his success as a playwright), when he did stick to the story purely as a well-told tale, he occasionally achieved the depth explored by one of his fellow contributors to *The Idler*, Guy de Maupassant. On reflection, it is a pity that Jerome didn't concentrate more on the short story and less on his occasional journalism. Possibly it was the very ease with which he was able to write humorous sketches that distracted him from delving deeper into the human condition, as does Maupassant at his best and most savage. There is very little savagery in Jerome, and only rarely did he court unpopularity in his views, such as those he proclaimed early in the First World War, while his friends and fellow writers Kipling and Wells were joining in the atavistic jingoism of the day, or on one occasion in the American south where he rounded on his audience and denounced a recent lynching. Curiously enough, he did pay lip service to the music-hall anti-Semitism of his day, though his friendship with his fellow-writer Israel Zangwill, who was a regular contributor to *The Idler*, belies this, and Jerome is remarkably percipient about the ideal State of Israel. Zangwill had confessed to Jerome that he had wasted half his life on Zionism.

'I never liked to say this to him,' Jerome wrote in *My Life and Times*, 'but it always seemed to me that the danger threatening Zionism is that it might be realized. Jerusalem was a Vision Splendid of the Jewish race—the Pillar of Fire that guided their footsteps across the centuries of shame and persecution. So long as it remained a dream, no Jew so poor, so hunted, so despised, but hugged to his breast his hidden birthright—his greatest inheritance he passed on to his children. Who in God's name wanted a third-rate provincial town on a branch of the Baghdad railway?' Seven Years after these words were published and six years after Jerome's death, Adolf Hitler came to power in Germany and the question was answered.

Jerome did try to get to grips with the questions of the day, the morality of war, and he had worked out his own relationship to the Church, which he had from childhood found unsatisfactory, in a revelatory way similar to that of Huckleberry Finn; and he had the concept of some insubstantial but omniscient deity, or God in man, which bordered on a kind of home-made Quakerism. Indeed, it was the Quakers who won his admiration while he was serving in France, when he said that but for them Christianity would have died.

On America, after his first flush of enthusiasm engendered by a profitable lecture tour, he turned such occasional spleen as he possessed.

'For spiritual progress, America seems to have no use,' he says. 'Every man in America has the right to think for himself so long as he thinks what he is told. If not, like the heretics in the Middle Ages—let him see to it that his chamber door is locked, that his tongue does not betray him. The Ku Klux Klan, with its travelling torture chamber, is but the outward and visible sign of modern America. America is not taking new wine, lest the old bottles be broken.'

Occasionally Jerome is aware of the approaching sentimentality that mars some of his justly forgotten excesses, such as *Paul Kelver* and *All Roads Lead to Calvary*, and he is able to step back from the brink and walk along the very edge of the precipice, as he does in the passages included here from his *Diary of a Pilgrimage*.

Jerome's trouble is that he was such a disparate, such a many-talented writer, who is remembered chiefly as the author of one delightfully funny book, *Three Men in a Boat*—which has been continuously in print for nearly a hundred years—and that this was followed by his next best-known work, *Three Men on the Bummel*, which is a failure by comparison. There is no question but that this latter work has done more harm to Jerome than anything else he wrote. But, happily, there is much more to Jerome than these two books, and perhaps I might be permitted to quote front Robert G. Logan who says, in his introduction to *Jerome K. Jerome: A Concise Bibliography*, albeit in a somewhat aggrieved tone: 'In compiling this list I have endeavoured to show something of the variety which is now little remembered.'

For my own part I hope the reader will come to appreciate Jerome K. Jerome, not only as a comic writer, but also as a thoughtful and entertaining guide to the awkward times through which he lived, with his first footsteps in the golden days before the First War and his last just before the conception of the Second, in a Europe whose bad seed festered out of sight.

MARTIN GREEN
August 1983

Birth and Parentage

I was born at Walsall in Staffordshire on 2 May, 1859. My father, at the time, was the owner of coal mines on Cannock Chase. They were among the first pits sunk on Cannock Chase; and are still referred to locally as the Jerome pits. My mother, whose name was Marguerite, was Welsh. She was the elder daughter of a Mr Jones, a solicitor of Swansea; and in those days of modest fortunes had been regarded as an heiress. It was chiefly with her money that the coal pits had been started. My mother's family were Nonconformists, and my father came of Puritan stock. I have heard my mother tell how she and her sister, when they were girls, would often have to make their way to chapel of a Sunday morning through showers of stones and mud. It was not until the middle of the century that the persecution of the Nonconformists throughout the country districts may be said to have entirely ceased. My father was educated at Merchant Taylors' School, and afterwards studied for an architect, but had always felt a 'call', as the saving is, to the ministry. Before his marriage, he had occupied his time chiefly in building chapels, and had preached in at least two of them. I think his first pulpit must have been at Marlborough. A silver salver in my possession bears the inscription: 'Presented to the Reverend Clapp Jerome by the congregation of the Independent Chapel, Marlborough, June 1828.' And at that time he could not have been much over one and twenty. From Marlborough he went to Cirencester. There he built the Independent chapel; and I see from a mighty Bible, presented to him by the 'Ladies of the Congregation,' that it was opened under his ministry on 6 June 1833. Altered out of all recognition, it is now the Cirencester Memorial Hospital on the road to the station. I have a picture of it as it appeared in my father's time. From an artistic point of view the world cannot be said to progress forwards.

On his marriage, my father settled down in Devonshire, where he farmed land at Appledore above Bideford; and also started a stone quarry. But the passion to be preaching never left him. In Devonshire, he preached whenever he got the chance, travelling about the country; but had no place of his own. When he gave up farming to go to Walsall, it was partly with the idea of making his fortune out of coal, and partly because a permanent pulpit had been offered him.

Sir Edward Holden, of Walsall, a still vigorous old gentleman of over ninety, with whom I dined not long ago, tells me my father was quite a wonderful preacher, and drew large congregations to Walsall from all round the district. He preached at first in the small Independent chapel that he found there. Later, the leading Nonconformists in the town got together, and the Congregational church in Bradford Street, which is still one of the features of the town, was built for him, my father giving his services as architect. It stands on the top of the hill, and in those days looked out over fields to Cannock Chase. It would be easy, as things turned out, for a wise man to point the obvious moral that if my father had followed sound biblical advice—had stuck to his preaching, for which God had given him the gift, and had left worldly enterprise to those apter in the ways of Mammon—it would, from every point of view, have been the better for him. But if success instead of failure had resulted, then he would no doubt have been praised as the ideal parent, labouring for the future welfare of his children. It was the beginning of the coal boom in Staffordshire, and fortunes were being made all round him, even by quite good men. In my father's case, it was the old story of the man who had the money calling in to his aid the man who had the experience. By the time my father had sunk his last penny, he knew all that was worth knowing about coal mining; but then it was too late. The final catastrophe seems to have been hastened by an inundation; and to cut a long story short, my father, returning home late one evening after the rest of the household were asleep, sat himself down on the edge of my mother's bed and broke to her, as gently as possible, the not unexpected news that he was a ruined man. I see from my mother's diary that the date coincides with the first anniversary of my birthday.

A few hundreds, all told, were perhaps saved out of the wreck. We moved into a small house in Stourbridge, nearby; and, having settled us there, my father, ever hopeful to the end, went off by himself to London, with the idea of retrieving our fortunes through the medium of the wholesale ironmongery business. He seems to have taken premises with a wharf in Narrow Street, Limehouse, and at the same time to have secured by way of residence the lease of a small house in Sussex Street, Poplar. He describes it, in his letters, as a corner house with a garden; and my mother seems to have pictured it as something rural. Poor lady! It must have been a shock to her when she saw it. Sometimes, when in the neighbourhood of the City, I jump upon an East Ham bus and, getting off at Stainsby Road, creep to the corner and peep round at it. I can understand my father finding one excuse after another for not sending for us. Of course he was limited by his means and the wish to be near his place of business in Narrow Street. Also, no doubt, he argued to himself that it would only be for a little while—until he could afford one of the fine Georgian houses in the East India Dock Road, where then lived well-to-do ship-owners and merchants. There, till we joined him two years later, my father lived by himself, limiting his household expenses to five shillings a week. For the ironmongery business was not prospering; and at Stourbridge there were seven of us in all to be kept. My mother did not know at the time—not till a friend betrayed him to her—and then she took matters into her own hands, and began her packing.

But before that, a deeper trouble than any loss of money had all but overwhelmed her. My little brother Milton had died after a short illness when six years old. A dear quaint little fellow he seems to have been: though maybe my mother's love exaggerated his piety and childish wisdom. On each anniversary of his death, she confides to her diary that she is a year nearer finding him again. The last entry, sixteen years afterwards and just ten days before she died herself, runs: 'Dear Milton's birthday. It can be now but a little while longer. I wonder if he will have changed.'

My brother's death left a gap in the family. My younger sister, Blandina, was eleven years older than myself; and Paulina, the elder, was a grown-up young woman with a Sunday School class and a sweetheart when I was still in frocks. The sweetheart was one Harry Beckett, an engineer. My mother at first entertained hopes of his conversion; but later seems to have abandoned them on learning that he had won in open competition the middleweight championship of Staffordshire. She writes him down sorrowfully as 'evidently little better than a mere prize fighter,' and I gather there were other reasons rendering him undesirable from my parents' point of view. The end, I know, was tears; and Harry departed for Canada. He turned up again in the 1880s and dropped in unexpectedly upon my sister. I happened to be staying with her at the time. She was then the mother of seven hefty boys and girls. A big handsome fellow he was still, with laughing eyes and kindly ways. I had taken to the writing of stories and was interested in the situation. He was doing well in the world; but he had never married. Perhaps he did mix his whisky and water with less water than there should have been as we sat together in the evening, we three—my brother-in-law was away up north on business—but as I watched them, I could not help philosophizing that life will always remain a gamble, with prizes sometimes for the imprudent, and blanks so often to the wise.

It is with our journey up to London, when I was four years old, that my memory takes shape. I remember the train and the fields and houses that ran away from me; and the great echoing cave at the end of it all—Paddington Station, I suppose. My mother writes that the house was empty when we reached it, the furniture not turning up till four days later. 'Papa and I and Baby slept in the house.' There must, of course, have been a little furniture, for my father had been living there. I remember their making me up a bed on the floor. And my father's and mother's talk, as they sat one each side of the fire, mingled with my dreams. 'Mrs Richard put up the two girls, and Fan and Mira slept at the Lashfords.' Eliza, I take it, must have been a servant. Aunt Fan was my mother's sister who lived with us: an odd little old lady with corkscrew curls and a pink and white complexion. The pictures of Queen Victoria as a girl always remind me of her.

My recollections are confused and crowded of those early days in Poplar. As I grew older I was allowed to wander about the streets a good deal by myself. My mother was against it, but my father argued that it was better for me. I had got to learn to take care of myself.

I have come to know my London well. Grim poverty lurks close to its fine thoroughfares, and there are sad, sordid streets within its wealthiest quarters. But about the East End of London there is a menace, a haunting terror that is to be found nowhere else. The awful silence of its weary streets. The ashen faces, with their lifeless eyes that rise out of the shadows and are lost. It was these surroundings in which I passed my childhood that gave to me, I suppose, my melancholy, brooding disposition. I can see the humorous side of things and enjoy the fun when it comes; but look where I will, there seems to me always more sadness than joy in life. Of all this, at the time, I was, of course, unconscious. The only trouble of which I was aware was that of being persecuted by the street boys. There would go up a savage shout if, by ill luck, I happened to be sighted. It was not so much the blows as the jeers and taunts that I fled from, spurred by mad terror. My mother explained to me that it was because I was a gentleman. Partly that reconciled me to it; and with experience I learned ways of doubling round corners and outstripping my pursuers; and when they were not actually in sight I could forget them. It was a life much like a hare must lead. But somehow he gets used to it, and there must be fine moments for him when he has outwitted all his enemies, and sits looking round him from his hillock, panting but proud.

My father had two nephews, both doctors, one living at Bow, and the other at Plaistow, which was then a country village. Bow was a residential suburb. One reached it by the Burdett Road. It was being built on then, but there were stretches where it still ran through scrubby fields and pastures. And beyond was Victoria Park, and the pleasant, old-world town of Hackney. Farther north still, one reached Stoke Newington, where dwelt grand folks that kept their carriage. I remember frequent visits to one such with my younger sister, Blandina. I see from my mother's diary that a mighty project was on foot: nothing less than the building of a new railway: from where to where, I cannot say. In the diary it is simply referred to as 'Papa's Railway.' For us it led from Poverty to the land of 'Heart's Desire.' I gather that the visits to Stoke Newington were in connection with this railway. Generally we were met at the great iron gates by a very old gentleman—or so he appeared to me—with a bald, shiny head and fat fingers. My sister was always the bearer of papers tied up with red tape, and these would be opened and spread out, and there would be talking and writing, followed by a sumptuous tea. Afterwards, taking my sister's hand in his fat fingers, he would tuck her arm through his and lead her out into the garden, leaving me supplied with picture books and sweets. My sister would come back laden with grapes and peaches, a present for Mamma. And whenever the weather was doubtful we were sent home in the deep-cushioned carriage with its prancing horses. Not to overexcite our neighbours of Sussex Street, it would stop at the end of the Burdett Road, and my sister and I would walk the rest of the way.

Our visits grew more and more frequent, and my mother's hopes for 'Papa's Railway' mounted higher and higher. Until one afternoon my sister came back out of the garden empty-handed, and with a frightened look in her eyes. She would not ride home in the carriage. Instead we walked very fast to Dalston junction, from where we took the train; and I could see that she was crying under her veil. It must have been an afternoon early in November. I remember his having asked my sister if she would like to see the Lord Mayor's Show. My mother writes in her diary under date 16 November, 'Papa's railway is not to be proceeded with. We are overwhelmed with sorrow. Every effort my dear husband makes proves unsuccessful. We seem shut out from the blessing of God.'

Even my father seems to have lost hope for a while. A page or two later I read, 'Dear Jerome has accepted a situation at Mr Rumbles.' A hundred a year from nine till eight. Feeling very low and sad.'

On 13 November, my mother tells Eliza that she can no longer afford to keep her. 'She wept and was very sorry to leave.'

'December 2nd. Jerome had his watch stolen. An elegant gold lever with his crest engraved that I gave him on our wedding day. Oh, how mysterious are God's dealings with us!'

On 4 December, the sun seems to have peeped out. 'Dear Blandina's birthday. Gave her my gold watch and a locket. She was very much delighted. Dear Pauline came home. A very pleasant, cheerful day, notwithstanding our heavy trials.' But early the following year it is dark again.

'January 12th. A very severe frost set in this week. Skating by torchlight in Victoria Park. Coals have risen eight shillings a ton. It is a fearful prospect. I have asked the Lord to remove it.

'January 18th. Today *suddenly*, to the surprise of all, a thaw began. The skating by torchlight all knocked on the head. Coals have gone down again just as we were at the last. "How much better are ye than many sparrows."'

My sisters seem to have taken situations from time to time. As governesses, I expect: the only calling then open to a gentlewoman. I read: 'Pauline to Ramsgate. Oh, how intensely do I wish we could all continue to live together!' And lower down on the same page 'Blanche to Mrs Turner's. Am feeling so lonely. The briars are too many for my feet to pass through; and the road is rough and dark.'

And then a week or two later, I likewise take my departure, but fortunately only on a brief visit to friends in the north of London. I am seen off at the station. My mother returns to the empty house and writes, 'Dear Luther went off delighted. Gracious Father, guard and protect my little lamb until he returns.'

Writing the word 'Luther' reminds me of an odd incident. I was called Luther as a boy, not because it was my name, but to distinguish me from my father, whose Christian name was also Jerome. A year or two ago, on Paddington platform, a lady stopped me and asked me if I were Luther Jerome. I had not heard the name for nearly half a century; and suddenly, as if I had been riding Mr Wells's Time Machine backwards, Paddington Station vanished with a roar (it may have been the pilot engine, bringing in the 6.15) and all the dead were living.

It turned out we had been playmates together in the old days at Poplar. We had not seen each other since we were children. She admitted, looking

17

closer at me, that there had come changes. But there was still 'something about the eyes,' she explained. It was certainly curious.

For some reason, about this time, there seems to have crept into my mother's heart the hope that we might get back possession of the farm in Devonshire to which my father had brought her home after their honeymoon, and that she might end her days there. It lies on the north side of the river above Bideford, and is marked by a ruined tower, near to which, years ago, relics were discovered proving beyond all doubt that the founder of our house was one Clapa, a Dane, who had obtained property in the neighbourhood about the year anno domini 1000. It was Clapa, I take it, who suggested our family crest, an upraised arm grasping a battle axe, with round about it the legend '*Deo omnia data.*' But as to how much Clapa owed to God and how much to his battle axe, found rusted beside his bones, history is silent. Be all this as it may, my mother never seems to have got over the idea that by some inalienable right the farm still belonged to us. Always she speaks of it as 'our farm.' Through the pages of her diary one feels her ever looking out towards it, seeing it as in a vision beyond the mean streets that closed her in, and among which in the end she died. One day she writes: 'Dear Jerome has told me about Norton and our farm. Why should it not be? With God all things are possible.' Later on, a large hamper arrives from Betsey, the farmer's wife. Betsey in my mother's time had been the dairymaid; and had married the carter. With the hamper, Betsey sends a letter containing further news concerning Norton—whoever or whatever 'Norton' may be. My mother writes: 'Well, God can restore even that to us. Oh, that I had more faith in God!'

Among all their troubles, one good thing seems to have been left to my father and mother: their love for one another. It runs through all the pages. There was a sad day when my sister Pauline lay dangerously ill. My mother returns from a visit to her.

'Gracious Father, sustain me that I may never distrust Thee, though wave follow wave in overwhelming succession. Came home with Papa, whose love is so constant and true. Mrs Cartwright sent some apples and a can of cream, and Mrs E. a pair of boots for Luther. "His mercy endureth for ever."'

'May 2nd, 1865. Dear little Luther's birthday. Six years old. Gave him a dove. Papa gave him *Robinson Crusoe.*'

About this time, and greatly to my mother's joy, I 'got religion,' as the saying is. I gave up taking sugar in my tea, and gave the twopence a week to the Ragged School in Threecolt Street. On Sundays, I used to pore over a great illustrated Bible and Foxe's *Book of Martyrs.* This used to be a popu-

lar book in religious houses, and children were encouraged to wallow in
its pictures of hideous tortures. Old Foxe may have meant well, but his
book makes for cruelty and lasciviousness. Also I worried myself a good
deal about Hell. I would suggest to our ecclesiastical authorities that they
should make up their mind about Hell and announce the result. When
I was a boy, a material Hell was still by most pious folks accepted as fact.
The suffering caused to an imaginative child can hardly be exaggerated.
It caused me to hate God, and later on, when my growing intelligence
rejected the conception as an absurdity, to despise the religion that had
taught it. It appeared one could avoid Hell by the simple process of 'believing'. But how was I to be sure that I did believe, sufficiently? There was
a mountain of rubbish on some waste land beside the Limehouse canal:
it was always spoken of locally as the 'mountain'. By way of experiment,
I prayed that this mountain might be removed. It would certainly have
been of advantage to the neighbourhood; and as, by comparison with
pictures I had seen, it was evidently but a very little mountain, I thought
my faith might be sufficient. But there it remained morning after morning, in spite of my long kneelings by my bedside. I felt the fault was mine
and despaired.

Another fear that haunted me was the Unforgivable Sin. If only one
knew what it was one might avoid it. I lived in terror of blundering into
it. One day—I forget what led to it—I called my Aunt Fan a bloody fool.
She was deaf and didn't hear it. But all that night I lay tossing on my bed.
It had come to me that this was the Unforgivable Sin, though even at the
time, and small though I was, I could not help reflecting that if this were
really so, there must in the parish of Poplar be many unforgivable sinners.
My mother, in the morning, relieved my mind as to its being the particular
Unforgivable Sin, but took it gravely enough notwithstanding, and kneel-
ing side by side in the grey dawn, we prayed for forgiveness.

I return to my mother's diary.

'Jan 1st, 1866. So time rolls on with its sorrows, conflicts, its unrealized
hopes. But these will pass away and be followed by the full, unmeasured
bliss of Eternity. Doctor Cumming prophesies this year to be our last.
He seems to overlook the second coming of Christ, with the glorious
ingathering of Jew and Gentile. Spent the evening with our friends in
Bedford Square. Enjoyed our visit very much.

'Jan. 31st. Old Wood made another proposal of marriage [to my sister
Blanche, I take it. Wood, no doubt, was the name of the bald-headed
old gentleman of Stoke Newington]. But God graciously preserved her

from being influenced by his wealth. Yet our path is very cloudy and full of sorrow.

'May 22nd. Peace meeting at Cannon Street Hotel. Papa made a beautiful speech. Caught cold coming home.

'June 7th, 1867. Our wedding day. Twenty-five years have passed since together we have borne the joys and sorrows, the mercies and trials of this weary way. But we can still say, "Hitherto hath the Lord helped us and preserved us." But oh, when will it be eventide with us? "And at eventide it shall be light."

'June 30th. 3.45 a.m., heard a queer noise. Came downstairs to ascertain the cause. A black and white cat sprang from the room. Dear little Fairy's cage was open, his feathers scattered all about. A thrill of anguish passed through me, and I called aloud in my sorrow. All came downstairs to mourn our loss. It was no use. We were all retiring, when a call from Luther made me rush downstairs again. In the drawing room there I beheld the little panting innocent clinging to the muslin curtains, and so delighted to pop once more into his cage. We were all now overjoyed and overwhelmed with astonishment at the bird's safety. How he escaped is a mystery. The Lord must have known how it would have grieved us all.

'July 18th. This morning we started to pay our long-talked-of visit to Appledore, and although we anticipated much pleasure, I had no idea of realizing half the kind attention and reception I and the dear children received. Everybody seemed to remember all my acts of kindness which I had long ago forgotten, and quite overwhelmed me with their love and affection. We enjoyed ourselves excessively. My visit has been to me like the refreshing rain after a long and dreary drought.'

To me, too, that visit was as a glimpse into another world. At Stourbridge, as a little chap, I must have seen something of the country. But I had forgotten it. Through the long journey, I sat with my face glued to the window. We reached Instow in the evening. The old ferryman came forward with a grin, and my mother shook hands with him, and all the way across they talked of strange names and places, and sometimes my mother laughed, and sometimes sighed. It was the first time I had been in a boat, and I was afraid, but tried to hide it. I stumbled over something soft, and it rose up and up until it was almost as tall as myself and looked at me. There must have been dogs in Poplar, but the few had never come my way, and anyhow nothing like this. I thought it was going to kill me and shut my eyes tight; but it only gave me a lick all over my face that knocked off my cap. The old ferryman swore at him, and he disappeared with a splash into the water. I thought he would be drowned and called out. But everybody laughed, and after all he wasn't, for I met him again the next day. A group of children was gathered on the shore, but instead of shouting or making faces at me they only looked at me with curious shy eyes, and my mother and sisters kissed them, and by this time quite a number of grown-ups had gathered round us. It was quite a time before we got away from them. I remember the walk up the steep hill. There were no lamps that I could see, but a strange light was all about us, as if we were in fairyland. It was the first time that I had ever climbed a hill. You had to raise your feet and bend your body. It was just as if someone were trying to pull you backwards. It all seemed very queer.

The days run into one another. I cannot separate them. I remember the line of reapers, bending above the yellow corn, and feeling sorry for it as it went down before their sickles. It was one evening when I had stolen away by myself that I found the moon. I saw a light among the treetops and thought at first to run home in fear, but something held me. It rose above the treetops higher and higher, till I saw it plainly. Without knowing why, I went down upon my knees and stretched out my arms to it. There always comes back to me that evening when I hear the jesting phrase 'wanting the moon.' I remember the sun that went down each night into the sea the other side of Lundy Island, and turned the farmhouse windows into blood. Of course he came to Poplar. One looked up sometimes and saw him there, but then he was sad and sick, and went away early in the afternoon. I had never seen him before looking bold and jolly. There were picnics on the topmost platform of the old, grey, ruined tower that still looks down upon the sea. And high teas in great farmhouses, and with old friends in Bideford, where one spread first apple jelly and then Devonshire cream upon one's bread, and lived upon squab pies and junkets, and quaffed sweet cider out of goblets, just like gods.

I got left behind on the way home—at Taunton, I think. We had got out of the train for light refreshment. My mother had thought my sisters were looking after me, and they had thought I was with her. It seemed to me unlikely we should ever meet again in spite of the assurances of a stout gentleman in gold buttons and a braided cap. But I remember con-solation coming to me with the reflection that here at least was interesting adventure, worthy of being recorded in my diary. For, unknown to all but my Aunt Fan, I was getting together material for a story of which I myself would be the hero. This notion of writing must have been my own entirely, for though my father could claim relationship with Leigh Hunt, I cannot remember hearing as a child any talk about literature. The stout gentleman with the gold buttons came back to me later, bringing a lady with him. She sat down beside me and guaranteed to take me back to my Mamma. There must have been something about her inviting confidence. I told her about the book, and how I was going to use for it this strange and moving incident. She greatly approved and was sure that I should succeed because I had the right idea. 'There is only one person you will ever know,' she told me. 'Always write about him. You can call him, of course, different names.'

By some magic, as it seemed to me, the kind lady and myself reached Paddington before my mother got there, so that, much to her relief, I was the first thing that she saw as she stepped out of the train. My mother hoped I had not been a trouble. But the kind lady assured her I had been most entertaining. 'I always find people interesting when they are talking about themselves,' the kind lady explained. And then she laughed and was gone.

Returning to our life in Poplar, things, I fancy, must have lightened a little, for a servant seems to have been engaged again. They come and go through the remainder of my mother's diary.

'Nov. 11th. Jane very rude, felt she was going to give me notice, so I gave her notice first. How different servants are to what they were!'

'Dec. 2nd. Jane left. Sarah came. Anyhow it can't be a change for the worse.'

It appears from an entry on 16 December 1868 that chiefly through the help of a Mr Halford I obtained a presentation to the Marylebone Grammar School, then called the Philological School, at the corner of Lisson Grove. I read: 'It has been an anxious time, but God has blessed dear Papa's efforts. The committee examined Luther this day, and the little lad passed through with flying colours. He will begin his school life in January. I must give up calling him Baby.'

So ends my childhood. It remains in my memory as quite a happy time. Not till years later did I learn how poor we were—of the long and bitter fight that my father and mother were waging against fate. To me it seemed we must be rather fortunate folk. We lived in the biggest house in Sussex Street. It had a garden round three sides of it with mignonette and nasturtiums that my mother watered of an evening. It was furnished more beautifully, I thought, than any house I had ever seen, with china and fine pictures and a semi-grand piano by Collard and Collard in the drawing room, and damask curtains to the windows. In the dining room were portraits of my father and mother by Muirhead, and when visitors came my mother would bring out the silver teapot and the old Swansea ware that she would never let anyone wash but herself. We slept on mahogany bedsteads, and in my father's room stood the Great Chest. The topmost drawer was always locked; but one day, when the proper time arrived, my father would open it, and then we should see what we would see. Even my mother confessed she did not know—for certain—what was hidden there. My father had been a great man and was going to be again. He wore a silk hat and carried a walking stick with a gold head. My mother was very beautiful, and sometimes, when she was not working, wore silks and real lace; and had an Indian shawl that would go through a wedding ring. My sisters could sing and play and always wore gloves when they went out. I had a best suit for Sundays and visitings; and always enough to eat. I see from my mother's diary that one of her crosses was that for a growing boy I was not getting proper nourishing food, but of this I had no inkling. There was a dish called 'bread and sop' which was sweet and warm and of which I was fond. For tea there would sometimes be golden syrup, and for supper bread with dripping spread quite thick. And on Sundays we had meat and pudding for dinner. If all things are as my mother so firmly believed, she has long known that her fears were idle—that notwithstanding, I grew up to be an exceptionally strong and healthy man. But I would that the foreknowledge could have come to her when she was living, and so have removed one, at least, of her many sorrows.

I Became an Actor

Among the sham agents must be classed the 'Professors,' or 'XYZs,' who are always 'able to place two or three' (never more than two or three: it would be no use four applying) 'lady and gentlemen amateurs, of tall or medium stature, either dark or fair, but must be of good appearance, at a leading West End theatre, in good parts: Salaried engagement.' These gentlemen are appreciative, and very quick to discern real talent. They perceived mine in a moment. They were all of them sure that I should make a splendid actor, and I was just the man they wanted. But they were conscientious. They scorned to hide the truth, and told me of my faults without reserve. They said that I was full of promise, that I had the makings of a really great actor in me, *but*—and the remarkable part of it was that no two of them agreed as to that 'but'. One said it was my voice. All that I wanted was to train my voice; then I should be perfect. Another thought my voice was a very fine one, but told me that my attitudes would not do at all. When my attitudes were a little more artistic, he could get me an engagement at once. A third, after hearing me recite a trifle or two from *Macbeth*, clapped me on the shoulder and insisted on shaking hands. There were tears almost in his eyes, and he appeared quite overcome. He said: 'My boy, you have got it in you. You are an actor! but—you want chic.'

I had not the slightest notion what he meant. I said: 'You think so.'

He was sure of it. It would be impossible for me to succeed without chic: *with* chic, I should soon be famous. I determined, at any price, to get chic, and I deferentially put it to him how he thought I could obtain it. He paused for a minute or so, evidently considering how it could be done, while I stood anxiously awaiting the result. Suddenly a bright idea seemed to strike him. He laid his hand confidentially on my arm, and in the impressive voice of a man who is communicating some extraordinary discovery, said: 'Come to me, twice a week, Tuesdays and Fridays, say, from eight to nine.' Then he drew back a few paces to see what effect it had upon me.

I replied that I supposed he meant he would teach it me. He seemed struck with my intelligence, and acknowledged that that was just precisely what he did mean. He explained—always in the same strictly confidential manner, as though he would not for the world have any one else know—that he had had great experience in this particular branch of dramatic education. He had letters now in his desk from well-known actors and actresses, persons of the greatest eminence, acknowledging that they owed their present position entirely to his teaching, and thanking him for all that he had done for them. He would show me those letters, and he rose to do so. But no, on second thoughts he would not; they were written in confidence, and it would not be right for him to let others see them—not even me, whom he felt he could trust. To do him justice, he never did show those letters, either to me, or, as far as I could learn, to any one else, though I subsequently came across three or four people who expressed an earnest desire to see them.

But I was slowly and painfully gaining experience, and I went away without leaving the five-pound note which I—'as a man of business'—ought to have seen was an absurdly small amount, his usual charge being twenty guineas; only, somehow or other, he had taken an interest in me, and felt sure I should reflect credit on his teaching, and so make it up to him in that way.

Another class that make a very good thing out of stage-struck asses, are the 'managers' (?) who have vacancies for 'an amateur lady and gentleman in a specially selected company.' They are men who evidently believe in the literal truth of Jaques' opinion as to all men and women being players, for they put raw novices into the leading parts with a confidence as to the result that is simply touching. The Thespian aspirant, who has never acted out of his own back parlour, feels a little nervous, though, at being cast for Banquo and Colonel Damas, to open with on the following Saturday. He cannot quite make up his mind whether a mistake has been made, a practical joke played upon him for the amusement of the rest of the company, or whether it is that the manager is really an intelligent man, who knows ability when he sees it. He does not like to speak about it, lest it should be thought he was not confident of his own powers—a failing of which the stage tyro is not usually guilty. Besides which, the parts might be taken from him, and this he by no means desires, although, at the same time, he is perfectly sure that he could play every other character in the piece much better. I had only one experience of the sham manager—at least, of this kind of sham manager. Unfortunately, there are other kinds, as most actors know to their cost, but these I have not come to yet. No, and I wish I had never gone to them, either.

There were about half a dozen of us noodles who had answered one advertisement, and we met every night for rehearsals at a certain house in Newman Street. Three or four well-known professionals, who were then starring in the provinces, but who would join us at the beginning of the next week, were to fill the chief parts, and we were to start for Gravesend immediately after their arrival. I had been engaged at a weekly salary of one pound fifteen shillings, and had been cast for the parts of Gilbert Featherstone in *Lost in London*, and the King in *Hamlet*. Everything went smoothly; there had been no suggestion of a premium or anything of that kind; and although I had, by this time, grown exceedingly suspicious, I began to think that this, at all events, was not a swindle. But I soon found out the trick. On the fifth night of the rehearsals, our manager was particularly pleasant, and complimented me on what he called my really original reading of the parts. During the pauses, he leant familiarly on my shoulder, and discussed the piece with me. We had a little argument about the part of the King. He differed from me, at first, on one or two points, but afterwards came round to my views, and admitted that I was right. Then he asked me how I was going to dress for the part. I had thought of this, even before I had studied the words, so I was as pat as could be on the subject, and we went through all the details, and arranged for a very gorgeous costume indeed. He did not try to stint me in the least, though I was once or twice afraid he might grumble at the cost. But no, he seemed quite as anxious as I was that the thing should be done in good style. It would be a little expensive, as he himself said, but then, 'you may just as well do the thing properly, while you are about it,' he added, and I agreed with him. He went on to reckon up the amount. He said that he could get the things very cheap—much cheaper than any one else—as he had a friend in the business, who would let him have them for exactly what they cost to make. I congratulated him on the fact, but, feeling no personal interest in the matter, began to be rather bored by his impressiveness on the subject. After adding it all up, he came to the conclusion that nine pounds ought to cover the lot.

'And very cheap, too,' said he. 'The things will be good, and will always come in useful,' and I agreed with him again, and remarked that I thought they would be well worth the money; but wondered what on earth all this had got to do with me.

Then he wanted to know whether I would pay the money that evening, or bring it with me next time.

'Me! Me pay!' I exclaimed, rendered ungrammatical by surprise. 'What for?'

'What for! Why, for the costume,' replied he. 'You can't play the part without, and if you got the things yourself, you'd have to pay about four pounds more, that's all. If you haven't got all the money handy,' he continued soothingly, 'let me have as much as you can, you know, and I'll try and get my friend to trust you for the rest.'

On subsequent inquiry among the others, I found that three of them had already let him have about five pounds each, and that a fourth intended to hand him over four pounds ten the following night. I and another agreed to wait and see. We did not see much, however. We never saw the well-known professionals, and, after the next evening, we never saw our manager again. Those who had paid saw less.

I now thought I would try hunting for myself, without the aid of agents or advertisements. I might be more successful, and certainly could not be less. The same friend that had recommended me not to write to the managers concurred with me in this view, and thought I could not do better than drop in occasionally at the Occidental; and I accordingly so dropped in. I suppose there is no actor who does not know the Occidental, though it does try to hide itself down a dark court, being, no doubt, of a retiring disposition, like the rest of the profession.

I found the company there genial and pleasant, and without any objection to drinking at my expense. When, however, I hinted my wish to join the profession, they regarded me with a look of the most profound pity, and seemed really quite concerned. They shook their heads gravely, told me their own experiences, and did all they could to dissuade me from my intention. But I looked upon them as selfish fellows who wanted to keep young talent from the stage. Even if their advice were given honestly, I argued, it was no use taking any notice of it. Everyone thinks his own calling the worst, and if a man waited to enter a profession until those already in it recommended him to, he might sit and twiddle his thumbs for the rest of his life. So I paid no attention to their warning, but continued in my course, and, at length, found someone to help me.

He was a large, flabby-looking individual, who seemed to live on Scotch whisky and big cigars, and was never either drunk or sober. He did not smell refreshing—a fact he made all the more impressive by breathing very hard, right into one's face, while talking. He had formerly been a country manager, but how he earned his livelihood now was always a mystery to me, as, although he rented a dirty little back room in a street leading out of the Strand,

and called it his office, he never did anything there but go to sleep. He was, however, well known to the theatrical frequenters of the Occidental—better known than respected, as I afterwards learnt—while he himself knew everybody, and it appeared to me that he was just the very man I wanted. At first, he was not any more enthusiastic than the others, but my mentioning that I was prepared to pay a small premium in order to obtain an appearance set him pondering, and, in the end, he didn't see why it could not be done. When I stated the figure I was ready to give, he grew more hopeful still, and came to the conclusion that it *could* be done. He did not even see why I should not make a big name, if I only left myself entirely in his hands.

'I have done the same thing for other people,' said he, 'and I can for you, if I like. There is ——,' he went on, getting talkative all at once, 'he is drawing his eighty pounds a week now. Well, damn it all, sir, I made that man—made him. He'd never have been anything more than a third-rate provincial actor, if it hadn't been for me. Then look at ——, at the ——, I knew him when he was having twenty-two shillings a week for responsibles, with old Joe Clamp, and that only when he could get it, mind you. I brought him up to London, started him at the Surrey, took him on to the West End, and worked him up to what he is. And now, when he passes me in his brougham, he don't know me,' and my new-found friend heaved a sigh, and took another pull to drown his grief at the ingratitude of human nature.

'Yes, sir,' he continued, on emerging from his glass, 'I made those men, and why shouldn't I make you?'

As I could not show any reason for his not doing so, he determined that he would; although he supposed that I should turn out just the same as the rest of them, and forget him when I was at the top of the tree. But I assured him most solemnly that I would not, and that I should be just as pleased to see him when I was a great man as I was then, and I shook hands warmly with him as a token of how pleased I was to see him then; for I felt really grateful to him for the favours he was going to bestow on me, and I was quite vexed that he should think I might prove ungrateful and neglect him.

When I saw him the next day, he told me he had done it. He had arranged an engagement for me with a Surrey side manager, to whom he would introduce me tomorrow, when the agreement could be signed, and everything settled. I was, accordingly, to be at his office for the purpose at eleven o'clock the following morning—and to bring the money with me. That was his parting injunction.

I did not walk back to my lodgings, I skipped back. I burst open the door, and went up the stairs like a whirlwind; but I was too excited to stop indoors. I went and had dinner at a first-class restaurant, the bill for which considerably lessened my slender means. 'Never mind,' I thought, 'what are a few shillings, when I shall soon be earning my hundreds of pounds.' I went to the theatre, but I don't know what theatre it was, or what was the play, and I don't think I knew at the time. I did notice the acting a little, but only to fancy how much better I could play each part myself. I wondered how I should like these particular actors and actresses when I came to know them. I thought I should rather like the leading lady, and, in my imagination, sketched out the details of a most desperate flirtation with her that would send all the other actors mad with jealousy. Then I went home to bed, and lay awake all night, dreaming.

I got up at seven the next morning and hurried over my breakfast, so as to be in time for the appointment at eleven. I think I looked at my watch (I wonder where that watch is, now!) at least every other minute. I got down to the Strand a little before ten, and wandered up and down a small portion of it, frightened to go a stone's throw from the office, and yet dreading to go too near it. I bought a new pair of gloves. I remember they were salmon colour, and one of them split as I was trying to get it on, so I carried it crumpled up in my hand and wore the other one. When it got within twenty minutes of the time, I turned into the street where the office was, and loitered about there, with an uncomfortable feeling that every one living in it knew what I had come about, and was covertly watching me from behind blinds and curtains. It seemed as though eleven o'clock never would come, but Big Ben tolled it out at last, and I walked to the door, trying to look as if I had just strolled up.

When I reached the office, no one was there, and the door was locked. My heart sank within me. Had the whole thing been a cruel hoax? Was it to be another disappointment? Had the manager been murdered? Had the theatre been burned down? Why were they not here? Something extraordinary must have happened to make them late on such an important occasion as this. I spent half an hour of intense suspense, and then they arrived. They hoped they had not kept me waiting, and I replied, 'Oh no, not at all,' and murmured something about having only just come myself.

As soon as we all three were inside the little office, I was introduced to the manager, who turned out to be an actor I had often seen on the boards, but who did not look a bit like himself, though he would have done very well for his own son; he was so much shorter and younger than he ought to have been. The clean-shaven face gives actors such a youthful appearance. It was difficult to believe, at first, that the sedate-looking boys I used to meet at rehearsal were middle-aged men with families, some of them.

Altogether, my future manager did not realize my expectations of him. He was not dressed with that reckless disregard for expense that I had looked for in a man of his position. To tell the truth, he presented a very seedy figure indeed. I put it down, however, to that contempt for outward appearance so often manifested by men of great wealth, and called to mind stories of millionaires who had gone about almost in rags; and I remembered, too, how I had once seen the mother of one of our leading burlesque actresses, and how I had been surprised at her extreme dinginess—the mother's.

They had the agreements all ready, and the manager and I signed in each other's presence, and exchanged. Then I handed him a ten-pound bank note, and he gave me a receipt for it. Everything was strictly formal. The agreement, especially, was very plain and precise, and there could be no mistake about it. It arranged for me to give my services for the first month gratis, and after that I was to receive a *salary according to ability*. This seemed to me very fair, indeed. If anything, it was, perhaps, a little reckless on his part, and one might press heavily upon him. He told me candidly, however, that he did not think I should be worth more than thirty shillings a week to him for the first two or three months, though, of course, it would depend upon myself entirely, and he should be only too pleased if it proved otherwise. I held a different opinion on the subject, but did not mention it, thinking it would be better to wait and let time prove it. So I merely said I wished for nothing but what was fair and just, and it appearing that this was exactly what he wanted me to have, we parted on the best of terms: but not before all particulars had been arranged. He was going to open for the summer season in three weeks' time, and the rehearsals were to commence about a fortnight before. For the next week, therefore, I was nothing; after that, I was an Actor!!!*

---

* My friends deny this. They say I never became an actor. I say I did, and I think I ought to know.

My Last Appearance

I left London exactly twelve months from the day on which I had started to fulfil my first provincial engagement, and I did not return to it again while I was an actor. I left it with my baggage early in the morning by the newspaper express from Euston; I returned to it late at night, footsore and hungry, and with no other possessions than the clothes I stood upright in.

Of the last few months of my professional life, the following brief extracts will speak. A slightly bitter tone runs through some of them, but at the time they were written I was suffering great disappointment, and everything was going wrong with me—circumstances under which a man is perhaps apt to look upon his surroundings through smoke-coloured glasses.

Three weeks after Christmas I write:

Business good and money regular. Business is almost always good, though, at pantomime time: the test will come later on, when we begin to travel. How a provincial audience does love a pantomime! and how I do hate it! I can't say I think very highly of provincial audiences. They need a lot of education in art. They roar over coarse buffoonery, and applaud noisy rant to the echo. One might as well go to Billingsgate to study English as to the provinces to learn acting.

I played First Low Comedy on Saturday night at half an hour's notice, the real First Low Comedy being hopelessly intoxicated at the time. It's a pity, amidst all the talk about the elevation of the stage, that the elevation of actors is not a less frequent occurrence. It can hardly improve the reputation of the profession in the eyes of the public, when they take up the *Era* and read advertisement after advertisement, ending with such lines as, 'None but sober people need apply.' 'Must contrive to keep sober, at all events during the performance.' 'People who are constantly getting drunk need not write.' I've known some idiots actually make themselves half tipsy on purpose before coming on the stage, evidently thinking, because they can't act when they've got all their few wits about them, that they'll manage better if they get rid of them altogether. There is a host of wonderful traditions floating about the theatrical world of this, that, and the other great actor having always played this, that, and the other part while drunk; and so, when some wretched little actor has to take one of these parts, he, fired by a noble determination to follow in the footsteps of his famous predecessor, gets drunk too.

Bad language is another thing that the profession might spare a lot of, and still have enough remaining for all ordinary purposes. I remember one night at —— we all agreed to fine ourselves a penny each time we swore. We gave it up after two hours' trial: none of us had any money left ...

Six weeks later:

Business gets worse instead of better. Our manager has behaved very well indeed. He paid us our salaries right up to the end of last week, though any one could see he was losing money every night; and then on Saturday, after treasury, he called us all together, and put the case frankly. He said he could not continue as he had been doing, but that, if we liked, he was ready to keep on with us for a week or two longer upon sharing terms, to see if the luck turned. We agreed to this, and so formed ourselves into what is called a 'commonwealth'—though common poverty would be a more correct term in my opinion, for the shares each night, after deducting expenses, have been about eighteen-pence. The manager takes three of these shares (one for being manager, one for acting, and the other one to make up the three), and the rest of us have one each. I'm getting awfully hard up, though I live for a week, now, on less than what I've often given for a dinner ...

A week later, this company broke up and I then joined another that was close handy at the time. It is from this latter that the following is written:

I just manage to keep my head above water, and that is all. If things get worse, I shall be done for. I've no money of my own left now.

A very sad thing happened here last week. Our leading man died suddenly from heart disease, leaving his wife and two children totally destitute. If he had been a big London actor, for half his life in receipt of a salary of, say, three thousand a year, the theatrical press would have teemed with piteous appeals to the public, all his friends would have written to the papers generously offering to receive subscriptions on his behalf; and all the theatres would have given performances at double prices to help pay his debts and funeral expenses. As, however, he had never earned anything higher than about two pounds a week, Charity could hardly be expected to interest herself about the case; and so the wife supports herself and her children by taking in washing. Not that I believe she would ask for alms, even were there any chance of her getting them, for, when the idea was only suggested to her, she quite fired up, and talked some absurd nonsense about having too much respect for her husband's profession to degrade it into a mere excuse for begging ...

This company also went wrong. It was a terrible year for theatres. Trade was bad everywhere, and 'amusements' was the very first item that people with diminishing incomes struck out of the list of their expenditure. One by one I parted with every valuable I had about me, and a visit to the pawnshop, just before leaving each town, became as essential as packing. I went through the country like a distressed ship through troubled waters, marking my track by the riches I cast overboard to save myself. My watch I left behind me in one town, my chain in another; a ring here, my dress suit there; a writing case I dropped at this place, and a pencil case at that. And so things went on—or, rather, off—till the beginning of May, when this letter, the last of the series, was written:

Dear Jim,—Hurrah! I've struck oil at last. I think it was time I did after what I've gone through. I was afraid the profession would have to do without me, but it's all safe now. I'm in a new company—joined last Saturday, and we're doing splendidly. Manager is a magnificent fellow, and a good man of business. He understands how to make the donkey go. He advertises and bills right and left, spares no expense, and does the thing thoroughly well. He's a jolly nice fellow, too, and evidently a man of intelligence, for he appreciates me. He engaged me without my applying to him at all, after seeing me act one night last week, when he was getting his company together. I play First Walking Gent at thirty-five shillings a week. He has been a captain in the army, and is a thorough gentlemen. He never bullies or interferes, and everybody likes him. He is going all round the north of England, taking all the big Lancashire and Yorkshire towns, and then going to bring us to London for the winter. He wants me to sign an agreement for one year certain at two pounds five. I haven't appeared to be too anxious. It's always best to hang back a bit in such cases, so I told him I would think it over; but of course

I shall accept. Can't write any more now. I'm just off to dine with him. We stop here three weeks, and then go to ———. Very comfortable lodgings. Yours, ———

That was written on Tuesday. On Saturday, we came to the theatre at twelve for treasury. The Captain was not there. He had gone that morning to pay a visit to Sir somebody or other, one of the neighbouring gentry, who was a great friend of his, and he had not yet returned. He would be back by the evening—so the courteous acting manager assured us—and treasury would take place after the performance.

So in the evening, when the performance was over, we all assembled on the stage, and waited. We waited about ten minutes, and then our Heavy Man, who had gone across the way to get a glass before they shut up, came back with a scared face to say that he'd just seen the booking clerk from the station, who had told him that the 'Captain' had left for London by an early train that morning. And no sooner had the Heavy Man made this announcement, than it occurred to the callboy that he had seen the courteous acting manager leave the theatre immediately after the play had begun, carrying a small black bag.

I went back to the dressing room, gathered my things into a bundle, and came down again with it. The others were standing about the stage, talking low, with a weary, listless air. I passed through them without a word, and reached the stage door. It was one of those doors that shut with a spring. I pulled it open, and held it back with my foot, while I stood there on the threshold for a moment, looking out at the night. Then I turned my coat collar up, and stepped into the street: the stage-door closed behind me with a bang and a click, and I have never opened another one since.

Silhouettes

Like most men who have the reputation of being funny—or of 'trying to be funny,' as the genial pressman would put it—I am myself a somewhat gloomily inclined personage. My own favourite reading is pessimistic poetry and stories of a pathetic or tragic tendency. The discovery that I was a humorist surprised me even more, I think, than it did my relations—even more, I think, than it did you, my dear cultured critic. While in the mood for confessing, I will acknowledge that I always fancied myself possessed of a pretty wit, together with humour in a mild and inoffensive degree; but my real strength, I told myself, lay in the direction of the tearful and the terrible. Had circumstances left me free to follow my natural bent, I should now be engaged in writing realistic novels, and plays almost gruesome enough for acceptance at the Independent Theatre.

I mention this in charity, hoping it may alleviate the sufferings of those who grieve because I write as I now do. They will be well advised not to stir me too deeply with their complainings. I do not like to seem to threaten, but, perhaps, it is only fair to them to state that I have, sketched out and stowed away in my desk, a six-act tragedy, and that it would not take very much to make me hunt it out and finish it.

My sympathies are always with the melancholy side of life and nature. I love the chill October days, when the brown leaves lie thick and sodden underneath your feet, and a low sound as of stifled sobbing is heard in the damp woods—the evenings in late autumn time, when the white mist creeps across the fields, making it seem as though old Earth, feeling the night air cold to its poor bones, were drawing ghostly bedclothes round its withered limbs. I like the twilight of the long grey street, sad with the wailing cry of the distant muffin man. One thinks of him, as strangely mitred, he glides by through the gloom, jangling his harsh bell, as the High Priest of the pale spirit of Indigestion, summoning the devout to come forth and worship. I find a sweetness in the aching dreariness of Sabbath afternoons in genteel suburbs—in the evil-laden desolateness of waste places by the river, when the yellow fog is stealing inland across the ooze and mud, and the black tide gurgles softly round worm-eaten piles. I love the bleak moor, when the thin long line of the winding road lies white on the darkening heath, while overhead some belated bird, vexed with itself for being out so late, scurries across the dusky sky, screaming angrily. I love the lonely, sullen lake, hidden away in mountain solitudes.

I suppose it was my childhood's surroundings that instilled in me this affection for sombre hues. One of my earliest recollections is of a dreary marshland by the sea. By day, the water stood there in wide, shallow pools. But when one looked in the evening they were pools of blood that lay there.

It was a wild, dismal stretch of coast. One day, I found myself there all alone—I forget how I managed it—and, oh, how small I felt amid the sky and the sea and the sandhills. I ran, and ran, and ran, but I never seemed to move; and then I cried, and screamed, louder and louder, and the circling seagulls screamed back mockingly at me. It was an 'unken' spot, as they say up north.

In the far back days of the building of the world, a long, high ridge of stones had been reared up by the sea, dividing the swampy grassland from the sand. Some of these stones—'pebbles,' so they called them round about—were as big as a man, and many as big as a fair-sized house; and when the sea was angry—and very prone he was to anger by that lonely shore, and very quick to wrath; often have I known him sink to sleep with a peaceful smile on his rippling waves, to wake in fierce fury before the night was spent—he would snatch up giant handfuls of these pebbles, and fling and toss them here and there, till the noise of their rolling and crashing could be heard by the watchers in the village afar off.

'Old Nick's playing at marbles tonight,' they would say to one another, pausing to listen. And then the women would close tight their doors, and try not to hear the sound.

Far out to sea, by where the muddy mouth of the river yawned wide, there rose ever a thin white line of surf, and underneath those crested waves there dwelt a very fearsome thing, called the Bar. I grew to hate and be afraid of this mysterious Bar, for I heard it spoken of always with bated breath, and I knew that it was very cruel to fisher folk, and hurt them so sometimes that

36

they would cry whole days and nights together with the pain, or would sit with white scared faces, rocking themselves to and fro.

Once when I was playing among the sandhills, there came by a tall, grey woman, bending beneath a load of driftwood. She paused when nearly opposite to me, and, facing seaward, fixed her eyes upon the breaking surf above the Bar. 'Ah, how I hate the sight of your white teeth,' she muttered; then turned and passed on.

Another morning, walking through the village, I heard a low wailing come from one of the cottages, while a little farther on a group of women were gathered in the roadway, talking. 'Ay,' said one of them, 'I thought the Bar was looking hungry last night.'

So, putting one and the other together, I concluded that the Bar must be an ogre, such as a boy reads of in books, who lived in a coral castle deep below the river's mouth, and fed upon the fishermen as he caught them going down to the sea or coming home.

From my bedroom window, on moonlight nights, I could watch the silvery foam, marking the spot beneath where he lay hid; and I would stand on tiptoe, peering out, until at length I would come to fancy I could see his hideous form floating below the waters. Then, as the little white-sailed boats stole by him, tremblingly, I used to tremble too, lest he should suddenly open his grim jaws and gulp them down; and when they had all safely reached the dark, soft sea beyond, I would steal back to the bedside, and pray to God to make the Bar good, so that he would give up killing and eating the poor fishermen.

Another incident connected with that coast lives in my mind. It was the morning after a great storm—great even for that stormy coast—and the passion-worn waters were still heaving with the memory of a fury that was dead. Old Nick had scattered his marbles far and wide, and there were rents and fissures in the pebbly wall such as the oldest fisherman had never known before. Some of the hugest stones lay tossed a hundred yards away, and the waters had dug pits here and there along the ridge so deep that a tall man might stand in some of them, and yet his head not reach the level of the sand.

Round one of these holes a small crowd was pressing eagerly, while one man, standing in the hollow, was lifting the few remaining stones off something that lay there at the bottom. I pushed my way between the straggling legs of a big fisher lad, and peered over with the rest. A ray of sunlight streamed down into the pit, and the thing at the bottom gleamed white. Sprawling there among the black pebbles it looked like a huge spider. One by one the last stones were lifted away, and the thing was left bare, and then the crowd looked at one another and shivered.

'Wonder how he got there,' said a woman at length. 'Somebody must ha' helped him.'

'Some foreign chap, no doubt,' said the man who had lifted off the stones, 'washed ashore and buried here by the sea.'

'What, six foot below the watermark, with all they stones a' top of him?' said another.

'That's no foreign chap,' cried a grizzled old woman, pressing forward. 'What's that that's aside him?'

Some one jumped down and took it from the stone where it lay glistening, and handed it up to her, and she clutched it in her skinny hand. It was a gold earring, such as fishermen sometimes wear. But this was a somewhat large one, and of rather unusual shape.

'That's young Abram Parsons, I tell you, as lies down there,' cried the old creature, wildly. 'I ought to know. I gave him the pair o' these forty year ago.'

It may be only an idea of mine, born of after brooding upon the scene. I am inclined to think it must be so, for I was only a child at the time, and would hardly have noticed such a thing. But it seems to my remembrance that as the old crone ceased, another woman in the crowd raised her eyes slowly, and fixed them on a withered, ancient man, who leant upon a stick, and that for a moment, unnoticed by the rest, these two stood looking strangely at each other.

From these sea-scented scenes, my memory travels to a weary land where dead ashes lie, and there is blackness—blackness everywhere. Black rivers flow between black banks; black, stunted trees grow in black fields; black withered flowers by black wayside. Black roads lead from blackness past blackness to blackness; and along them trudge black, savage-looking men and women; and by them black, old-looking children play grim, unchildish games.

When the sun shines on this black land, it glitters black and hard; and when the rain falls a black mist rises towards heaven, like the hopeless prayer of a hopeless soul.

By night it is less dreary, for then the sky gleams with a lurid light, and out of the darkness the red flames leap, and high up in the air they gambol and writhe—the demon spawn of that evil land, they seem.

Visitors who came to our house would tell strange tales of this black land, and some of the stories I am inclined to think were true. One man said he saw a young bulldog fly at a boy and pin him by the throat. The lad jumped about with much sprightliness, and tried to knock the dog away. Whereupon the boy's father rushed out of the house, hard by, and caught his son and heir roughly by the shoulder. 'Keep still, thee young —— can't 'ee,' shouted the man angrily. 'Let 'un taste blood.'

Another time, I heard a lady tell how she had visited a cottage during a strike, to find the baby, together with the other children, almost dying for want of food. 'Dear, dear me,' she cried, taking the wee wizened mite from the mother's arms, 'but I sent you down a quart of milk, yesterday. Hasn't the child had it?'

'Theer weer a little coom, thank 'ee kindly, ma'am,' the father took upon himself to answer, 'but thee see it weer only just enow for the poops.'

We lived in a big lonely house on the edge of a wide common. One night, I remember, just as I was reluctantly preparing to climb into bed, there came a wild ringing at the gate, followed by a hoarse, shrieking cry, and then a frenzied shaking of the iron bars.

Then hurrying footsteps sounded through the house, and the swift opening and closing of doors; and I slipped back hastily into my knickerbockers and ran out. The womenfolk were gathered on the stairs, while my father stood in the hall, calling to them to be quiet. And still the wild ringing of the bell continued, and, above it, the hoarse, shrieking cry.

My father opened the door and went out, and we could hear him striding down the gravel path, and we clung to one another and waited.

After what seemed an endless time, we heard the heavy gate unbarred, and quickly clanged to, and footsteps returning on the gravel. Then the door opened again, and my father entered, and behind him a crouching figure that felt its way with its hands as it crept along, like a blind man might. The figure stood up when it reached the middle of the hall, and mopped its eyes with a dirty rag that it carried in its hand; after which it held the rag over the umbrella stand and wrung it out, as washerwomen wring out clothes, and the dark drippings fell into the tray with a dull, heavy splut.

My father whispered something to my mother, and she went out towards the back; and, in a little while, we heard the stamping of hoofs—the angry plunge of a spur-startled horse—the rhythmic throb of the long, straight gallop, dying away into the distance.

My mother returned and spoke some reassuring words to the servants. My father, having made fast the door and extinguished all but one or two of the lights, had gone into a small room on the right of the hall; the crouching figure, still mopping that moisture from its eyes, following him. We could hear them talking there in low tones, my father questioning, the other voice thick and interspersed with short panting grunts.

We on the stairs huddled closer together, and, in the darkness, I felt my mother's arm steal round me and encompass me, so that I was not afraid. Then we waited, while the silence round our frightened whispers thickened and grew heavy till the weight of it seemed to hurt us.

At length, out of its depths, there crept to our ears a faint murmur. It gathered strength like the sound of the oncoming of a wave upon a stony shore, until it broke in a Babel of vehement voices just outside. After a few moments, the hubbub ceased, and there came a furious ringing—then angry shouts demanding admittance.

Some of the women began to cry. My father came out into the hall, closing the room door behind him, and ordered them to be quiet, so sternly that they were stunned into silence. The furious ringing was repeated; and, this time, threats mingled among the hoarse shouts. My mother's arm tightened around me, and I could hear the beating of her heart.

The voices outside the gate sank into a low confused mumbling. Soon they died away altogether, and the silence flowed back.

My father turned up the hall lamp, and stood listening.

Suddenly, from the back of the house, rose the noise of a great crashing, followed by oaths and savage laughter.

My father rushed forward, but was borne back; and, in an instant, the hall was full of grim, ferocious faces. My father, trembling a little (or else it was the shadow cast by the flickering lamp), and with lips tight pressed, stood confronting them; while we women and children, too scared even to cry, shrank back up the stairs.

What followed during the next few moments is, in my memory, only a confused tumult, above which my father's high, clear tones rise every now and again, entreating, arguing, commanding. I see nothing distinctly until one of the grimmest of the faces thrusts itself before the others, and a voice which, like Aaron's rod, swallows up all its fellows, says in deep, determined bass, 'Coom, we've had enow chatter, master. Thee mun give 'un up, or thee mun get out o' th' way an' we'll search th' house for oursel'.'

Then a light flashed in my father's eyes that kindled something inside me, so that the fear went out of me, and I struggled to free myself from my mother's arm, for the desire stirred me to fling myself down upon the grimy faces below, and beat and stamp upon them with my fists. Springing across the hall, he snatched from the wall where it hung an ancient club, part of a trophy of old armour, and planting his back against the door through which they would have to pass, he shouted, 'Then be damned to you all, he's in this room. Come and fetch him out.'

(I recollect that speech well. I puzzled over it, even at that time, excited though I was. I had always been told that only low, wicked people ever used the word 'damn,' and I tried to reconcile things, and failed.)

The men drew back and muttered among themselves. It was an ugly-looking weapon, studded with iron spikes. My father held it secured to his hand by a chain, and there was an ugly look about him also, now, that gave his face a strange likeness to the dark faces round him.

But my mother grew very white and cold, and underneath her breath she kept crying, 'Oh, will they never come—will they never come?' and a cricket somewhere about the house began to chirp.

Then all at once, without a word, my mother flew down the stairs, and passed like a flash of light through the crowd of dusky figures. How she did it I could never understand, for the two heavy bolts had both been drawn, but the next moment the door stood wide open; and a hum of voices, cheery with the anticipation of a period of perfect bliss, was borne in upon the cool night air.

My mother was always very quick of hearing.

Again, I see a wild crowd of grim faces, and my father's, very pale, amongst them. But this time the faces are very many, and they come and go like faces in a dream. The ground beneath my feet is wet and sloppy, and a black rain is falling. There are women's faces in the crowd, wild and haggard, and long skinny arms stretch out threateningly towards my father, and shrill, frenzied voices call out curses on him. Boys' faces also pass me in the grey light, and on some of them there is an impish grin.

I seem to be in everybody's way, and, to get out of it, I crawl into a dark, draughty corner and crouch there among cinders. Around me, great engines fiercely strain and pant like living things fighting beyond their strength. Their gaunt arms whirl madly above me, and the ground rocks with their throbbing. Dark figures flit to and fro, pausing from time to time to wipe the black sweat from their faces.

The pale light fades, and the flame-lit night lies red upon the land. The flitting figures take strange shapes. I hear the hissing of wheels, the furious clanking of iron chains, the hoarse shouting of many voices, the hurrying tread of many feet; and through all the wailing and weeping and cursing that never seem to cease. I drop into a restless sleep, and dream that I have broken a chapel window, stone-throwing, and have died and gone to hell.

At length, a cold hand is laid upon my shoulder and I awake. The wild faces have vanished, and all is silent now, and I wonder if the whole thing has been a dream. My father lifts me into the dogcart, and we drive home through the chill dawn.

My mother opens the door softly as we alight. She does not speak, only looks her question. 'It's all over, Maggie,' answers my father very quietly, as he takes off his coat and lays it across a chair. 'We've got to begin the world afresh.'

My mother's arms steal up about his neck; and I, feeling heavy with a trouble I do not understand, creep off to bed.

Variety Patter

My first appearance at a music hall was in the year of grace one thousand eight hundred and s—— Well, I would rather not mention the exact date. I was fourteen at the time. It was during the Christmas holidays, and my aunt had given me five shillings to go and see Phelps—I think it was Phelps—in *Coriolanus*—I think it was *Coriolanus*. Anyhow, it was to see a high-class and improving entertainment, I know.

I suggested that I should get young Skegson, who lived in our road, to go with me. Skegson is a barrister now, and could not tell you the difference between a knave of clubs and a club of knaves. A few years hence, he will, if he works hard, be innocent enough for a judge. But at the period of which I speak he was a red-haired boy of worldly tastes, notwithstanding which I loved him as a brother. My dear mother wished to see him before consenting to the arrangement, so as to be able to form her own opinion as to whether he was a fit and proper companion for me; and, accordingly, he was invited to tea. He came, and made a most favourable impression upon both my mother and my aunt. He had a way of talking about the advantages of application to study in early life, and the duties of youth towards those placed in authority over it, that won for him much esteem in grownup circles. The spirit of the Bar had descended upon Skegson at a very early period of his career.

My aunt, indeed, was so much pleased with him that she gave him two shillings towards his own expenses ('sprung half a dollar' was how he put it when we got outside), and commended me to his especial care.

Skegson was very silent during the journey. An idea was evidently maturing in his mind. When we reached the Angel, he stopped and said: 'Look here, I'll tell you what we'll do. Don't let's go and see that rot. Let's go to a music hall.'

I gasped for breath. I had heard of music halls. A stout lady had denounced them across our dinner table on one occasion, fixing the while a steely eye upon her husband, who sat opposite and seemed uncomfortable, as low, horrid places, where people smoked and drank, and wore short skirts, and had added an opinion that they ought to be put down by the police—whether the skirts or the halls she did not explain. I also recollected that our charwoman, whose son had lately left London for a protracted stay in Devonshire, had, in conversation with my mother, dated his downfall from the day when he first visited one of these places; and likewise that Mrs Philcox's nursemaid, upon her confessing that she had spent an evening at one with her young man, had been called a shameless hussy, and summarily dismissed as being no longer a fit associate for the baby.

But the spirit of lawlessness was strong within me in those days, so that I hearkened to the voice of Skegson, the tempter, and he lured my feet from the paths that led to virtue and Sadlers Wells, and we wandered into the broad and crowded ways that branch off from the Angel towards merry Islington.

Skegson insisted that we should do the thing in style, so we stopped at a shop near the Agricultural Hall and purchased some big cigars. A huge card in the window claimed for these that they were 'the most satisfactory twopenny smoke in London.' I smoked two of them during the evening, and never felt more satisfied—using the word in its true sense, as implying that a person has had enough of a thing, and does not desire any more of it, not just then—in all my life. Where we went, and what we saw when we got there, my memory is not very clear about: it never was. We sat at a little marble table. I know it was marble because it was so hard and cool to the head. From out of the smoky mist a ponderous creature of strange, unde-fined shape, floated heavily towards us, and deposited a squat tumbler in front of me containing a pale yellowish liquor, which subsequent investiga-tion has led me to believe must have been Scotch whisky. It seemed to me then the most nauseous stuff I had ever swallowed. It is curious to look back and notice how one's tastes change.

I reached home very late and very sick. That was my first dissipation, and, as a lesson, it has been of more practical use to me than all the good books and sermons in the world could have been. I can remember to this day standing in the middle of the room in my nightshirt, trying to catch my bed as it came round.

Next morning I confessed everything to my mother, and, for several months afterwards, was a reformed character. Indeed, the pendulum of my conscience swung too far the other way, and I grew exaggeratedly remorseful and unhealthily moral.

There was published in those days, for the edification of young people, a singularly pessimistic periodical, entitled the *Children's Band of Hope Review*. It was a magazine much in favour among grown-up people, and a bound copy of vol. IX had lately been won by my sister as a prize for punctuality. (I fancy she must have exhausted all the virtue she ever possessed, in that direction, upon the winning of that prize. At all events, I have noticed no ostentatious display of the quality in her later life.) I had formerly expressed contempt for this book, but now, in my regenerate state, I took a morbid pleasure in poring over its denunciations of sin and sinners. There was one picture in it that appeared peculiarly applicable to myself. It represented a gaudily costumed young man, standing on the topmost of three steep steps, smoking a large cigar. Behind him was a very small church, and below, a bright and not altogether uninviting looking hell. The picture was headed 'The Three Steps to Ruin,' and the three stairs were labelled respectively 'Smoking', 'Drinking', 'Gambling'. I had already travelled two thirds of the road! Was I going all the way, or should I be able to get back? I used to lie awake at night and think about it, till I grew half crazy.

Alas! since then I have completed the descent, so where my future will be spent I do not care to think.

Another picture in the book that troubled me was the frontispiece. This was a highly coloured print, illustrating the broad and narrow ways. The narrow way led upward past a Sunday school and a lion to a city in the clouds. This city was referred to in the accompanying letterpress as a place of 'Rest and Peace', but in as much as the town was represented in the illustration as surrounded by a perfect mob of angels, each one blowing a trumpet twice his own size, and obviously blowing it for all he was worth, a certain confusion of ideas would seem to have crept into the allegory.

The other path—the 'broad way'—which ended in what at first glance appeared to be a highly successful display of fireworks, started from the door of a tavern, and led past a music hall, on the steps of which stood a gentleman smoking a cigar. (All the wicked people in this book smoked cigars—all except one young man who had killed his mother and died raving mad. He had gone astray on short pipes.)

This made it uncomfortably clear to me which direction I had chosen, and I was greatly alarmed, until, on examining the picture more closely, I noticed, with much satisfaction, that about midway the two paths were connected by a handy little bridge, by the use of which it seemed feasible, starting on the one path and ending up on the other, to combine the practical advantages of both roads.

My belief in the possibility of this convenient compromise must, I fear, have led to an ethical relapse, for there recurs to my mind a somewhat painful scene of a few months' later date in which I am seeking to convince a singularly unresponsive landed proprietor that my presence in his orchard is solely and entirely due to my having unfortunately lost my way.

It was not until I was nearly seventeen that the idea occurred to me to visit a music hall again. Then, having regard to my double capacity of 'Man About Town' and journalist (for I had written a letter to the *Era*, complaining of the way pit doors were made to open, and it had been inserted), I felt I had no longer any right to neglect acquaintanceship with so important a feature in the life of the people. Accordingly, one Saturday night, I wended my way to the 'Pav'; and there the first person that I ran against was my uncle. He laid a heavy hand upon my shoulder, and asked me, in severe tones, what I was doing there. I felt this to be an awkward question, for it would have been useless trying to make him understand my real motives (one's own relations are never sympathetic), and I was somewhat nonplussed for an answer, until the reflection occurred to me: what was he doing there? This riddle I, in my turn, propounded to him, with the result that we entered into treaty by the terms of which it was agreed that no future reference should be made to the meeting by either of us—at least, not in the presence of any member of the family—and the compact was ratified according to the usual custom, my uncle paying the necessary expenses.

In those days, we sat, some four or six of us, round a little table, on which were placed our drinks. Now we have to balance them upon a narrow ledge; and ladies, as they pass, dip the ends of their cloaks into them, and gentlemen stir them up for us with the ferrules of their umbrellas, or else sweep them off into our laps with their coat tails, saying as they do so, 'Oh, I beg your pardon.'

Also, in those days, there were 'chairmen'—affable gentlemen, who would drink anything at anybody's expense, and drink any quantity of it, and never seem to get any fuller. I was introduced to a music hall chairman once, and when I said to him, 'What is your drink?' he took up the 'list of beverages' that lay before him, and, opening it, waved his hand lightly across its entire contents, from clarets, past champagnes and spirits, down to liqueurs. 'That's my drink, my boy,' said he. There was nothing narrow-minded or exclusive about his tastes.

It was the chairman's duty to introduce the artists. 'Ladies and gentle-men,' he would shout, in a voice that united the musical characteristics of a foghorn and a steam saw, 'Miss 'Enerietta Montressor, the popular serio-comic, will now happear.' These announcements were invariably received with great applause by the chairman himself, and generally with chilling indifference by the rest of the audience.

It was also the privilege of the chairman to maintain order, and rep-rimand evil-doers. This he usually did very effectively, employing for the purpose language both fit and forcible. One chairman that I remember, seemed, however, to be curiously deficient in the necessary qualities for this part of his duty. He was a mild and sleepy little man, and, unfortunately, he had to preside over an exceptionally rowdy audience at a small hall in the southeast district. On the night that I was present, there occurred a great disturbance. 'Joss Jessop, the Monarch of Mirth,' a gentleman evidently high in local request, was, for some reason or other, not forthcoming, and, in his place, the management proposed to offer a female performer on the zither, one Signorina Ballatino.

The little chairman made the announcement in a nervous, deprecatory tone, as if he were rather ashamed of it himself. 'Ladies and gentlemen,' he began. (The poor are staunch sticklers for etiquette. I overheard a small child explaining to her mother one night in Threecolts Street, Limehouse, that she could not get into the house because there was a 'lady' on the doorstep, drunk.) 'Signorina Ballatino, the world-renowned—'

Here a voice from the gallery requested to know what had become of 'Old Joss,' and was greeted by loud cries of ''Ere, 'ere.' The chairman, ignor-ing the interruption, continued: '—the world-renowned performer on the zither—'

'On the whoter?' came in tones of plaintive inquiry from the back of the hall.

'*Hon* the zither,' retorted the chairman, waxing mildly indignant; he meant zithern, but he called it a zither. 'A hinstrument well known to any-body as 'as 'ad any learning.'

This sally was received with much favour, and a gentleman who claimed to be acquainted with the family history of the interrupter begged the chairman to excuse him on the grounds that his (the interrupter's) mother used to get drunk with the twopence a week and never sent him to school.

Cheered by this breath of popularity, our little president endeavoured to complete his introduction of the Signorina. He again repeated that she was the world-renowned performer on the zither; and, undeterred by the audible remark of a lady in the pit to the effect that she'd 'never 'eard on 'er,' added: 'She will now, ladies and gentlemen, with your kind permission, give you examples of the—'

'Blow yer zither,' here cried out the gentleman who had started the agitation, 'we want Joss Jessop.'

This was the signal for much cheering and shrill whistling, in the midst of which a wag with a piping voice suggested as a reason for the favourite's non-appearance that he had not been paid his last week's salary.

A temporary lull occurred at this point, and the chairman, seizing the opportunity to complete his oft-impeded speech, suddenly remarked, '— songs of the Sunny South;' and immediately sat down and began hammering upon the table.

Then Signora Ballatino, clothed in the costume of the Sunny South, where clothes are less essential than in these colder climes, skipped airily forward, and was most ungallantly greeted with a storm of groans and hisses. Her beloved instrument was unfeelingly alluded to as a pie dish, and she was advised to take it back and get the penny on it. The chairman, addressed by his Christian name of 'Jimmee', was told to lie down and let her sing him to sleep. Every time she attempted to start playing, shouts were raised for Joss.

At length the chairman, overcoming his evident disinclination to take any sort of hand whatever in the game, rose and gently hinted at the desirability of silence. The suggestion not meeting with any support, he proceeded to adopt sterner measures. He addressed himself personally to the ringleader of the rioters, the man who had first championed the cause of the absent Joss. This person was a brawny individual, who judging from appearance, followed in his business hours the calling of a coal-heaver. 'Yes, sir,' said the chairman, pointing a finger towards him, where he sat in the front row of the gallery, 'you, sir, in the flannel shirt. I can see you. Will you allow this lady to give her entertainment?'

'No,' answered he of the coal-heaving profession, in stentorian tones.

'Then, sir,' said the little chairman, working himself up into a state suggestive of Jove about to launch a thunderbolt,—'then, sir, all I can say is that you are no gentleman.'

This was a little too much, or rather a good deal too little, for the Signora Ballatino. She had hitherto been standing in a meek attitude of pathetic appeal, wearing a fixed smile of ineffable sweetness; but she evidently felt that she could go a bit farther than that herself, even if she was a lady. Calling the chairman 'an old messer,' and telling him for —— sake to shut up if that was all he could do for his living, she came down to the front, and took the case into her own hands.

She did not waste time on the rest of the audience. She went direct for that coal-heaver, and thereupon ensued a slanging match the memory of which sends a thrill of admiration through me even to this day. It was a battle worthy of the gods. He was a heaver of coals, quick and ready beyond his kind. During many years' sojourn east and south, in the course of many wanderings from Billingsgate to Limehouse Hole, from Petticoat Lane to Whitechapel Road; out of eelpie shop and penny gaff; out of tavern and street, and court and doss-house, he had gathered together slang words and terms and phrases, and they came back to him now, and he stood up against her manfully.

But as well might the lamb stand up against the eagle, when the shadow of its wings falls across the green pastures, and the wind flies before its dark oncoming. At the end of two minutes he lay gasping, dazed and speechless.

Then she began.

She announced her intention of 'wiping down the bloomin' 'all' with him, and making it respectable; and, metaphorically speaking, that is what she did. Her tongue hit him between the eyes, and knocked him down and trampled on him. It curled round and round him like a whip, and then it uncurled and wound the other way. It seized him by the scruff of his neck, and tossed him up into the air, and caught him as he descended, and flung him to the ground, and rolled him on it. It played around him like forked lightning, and blinded him. It danced and shrieked about him like a host of whirling fiends, and he tried to remember a prayer, and could not. It touched him lightly on the sole of his foot and the crown of his head, and his hair stood up straight, and his limbs grew stiff. The people sitting near him drew away, not feeling it safe to be near, and left him alone, surrounded by space, and language.

It was the most artistic piece of work of its kind that I have ever heard. Every phrase she flung at him seemed to have been woven on purpose to entangle him and to embrace in its choking folds his people and his gods, to strangle with its threads his every hope, ambition and belief. Each term she put upon him clung to him like a garment, and fitted him without a crease. The last name that she called him one felt to be, until one heard the next, the one name that he ought to have been christened by.

For five and three-quarter minutes by the clock she spoke, and never for one instant did she pause or falter; and in the whole of that onslaught there was only one weak spot.

That was when she offered to make a better man than he was out of a Guy Fawkes and a lump of coal. You felt that one lump of coal would not have been sufficient.

At the end, she gathered herself together for one supreme effort, and hurled at him an insult so bitter with scorn, so sharp with insight into his career and character, so heavy with prophetic curse, that strong men drew and held their breath while it passed over them, and women hid their faces and shivered.

Then she folded her arms, and stood silent; and the house, from floor to ceiling, rose and cheered her until there was no more breath left in its lungs.

In that one night she stepped from oblivion into success. She is now a famous 'artiste'.

But she does not call herself Signora Ballatino, and she does not play upon the zithern. Her name has a homelier sound, and her speciality is the delineation of coster character.

The Servant Girl

There are two types of servant girl to be met with on the stage. This is an unusual allowance for one profession.

There is the lodging-house slavey. She has a good heart, and a smutty face, and is always dressed according to the latest fashion in scarecrows.

Her leading occupation is the cleaning of boots. She cleans boots all over the house, at all hours of the day. She comes and sits down on the hero's breakfast table, and cleans them over the poor fellow's food. She comes into the drawing room cleaning boots.

She has her own method of cleaning them, too. She rubs off the mud, puts on the blacking, and polishes up all with the same brush. They take an enormous amount of polishing, she seems to do nothing else all day long but walk about shining one boot, and she breathes on it and rubs it till you wonder there is any leather left, yet it never seems to get any brighter, nor, indeed, can you expect it to, for when you look closely you see it is a patent leather boot that she has been throwing herself away upon all this time.

Somebody has been having a lark with the poor girl. The lodging-house slavey brushes her hair with the boot brush, and blacks the end of her nose with it.

We were acquainted with a lodging-house slavey once—a real one, we mean. She was the handmaiden at a house in Bloomsbury, where we once hung out. She was untidy in her dress, it is true, but she had not quite that castaway and gone-to-sleep-in-a-dustbin appearance that we, an earnest student of the drama, felt she ought to present, and we questioned her one day on the subject.

'How is it, Sophronia,' we said, 'that you distantly resemble a human being instead of giving one the idea of an animated rag shop? Don't you ever polish your nose with the blacking brush, or rub coal into your head, or wash your face in treacle, or put skewers into your hair, or anything of that sort, like they do on the stage?'

She said, 'Lord love you, what should I want to go and be a bally idiot like that for?'

And we have not liked to put the question elsewhere since then.

The other type of servant girl on the stage—the villa servant girl—is a very different personage. She is a fetching little thing, and dresses bewitchingly, and is always clean. Her duties are to dust the legs of the chairs in the drawing room. That is the only work she ever has to do, but it must be confessed she does that thoroughly. She never comes into the room without dusting the legs of these chairs, and she dusts them again before she goes out.

If anything ought to be free from dust in a stage house, it should be the legs of the drawing-room chairs.

She is going to marry the manservant, is the stage servant girl, as soon as they have saved up sufficient out of their wages to buy a hotel. They think they will like to keep a hotel. They don't understand a bit about the business, which we believe is a complicated one, but this does not trouble them in the least.

They quarrel a good deal over their love-making, do the stage servant girl and her young man, and they always come into the drawing room to do it. They have got the kitchen, and there is the garden (with a fountain and mountains in the background—you can see it through the window), but no! no place in or about the house is good enough for them to quarrel in except the drawing room. They quarrel there so vigorously that it even interferes with the dusting of the chair legs.

She ought not to be long in saving up sufficient to marry on, for the generosity of people on the stage to the servants there makes one seriously consider the advisability of ignoring the unremunerative professions of ordinary life, and starting a new and more promising career as a stage servant.

No one ever dreams of tipping the stage servant with *less* than a sovereign when they ask her if her mistress is at home, or give her a letter to post, and there is quite a rush at the end of the piece to stuff five-pound notes into her hand. The good old man gives her ten.

The stage servant is very impudent to her mistress, and the master—he falls in love with her, and it does upset the house so.

Sometimes the servant girl is good and faithful, and then she is Irish. All good servant girls on the stage are Irish.

All the male visitors are expected to kiss the stage servant girl when they come into the house, and to dig her in the ribs, and to say, 'Do you know, Jane, I think you're an uncommonly nice girl—click.' They always say this, and she likes it.

Many years ago, when we were young, we thought we would see if things were the same off the stage, and the next time we called at a certain friend's house, we tried this business on.

She wasn't *quite* so dazzlingly beautiful as they are on the stage, but we passed that. She showed us up into the drawing room, and then said she would go and tell her mistress we were there.

We felt this was the time to begin. We skipped between her and the door. We held our hat in front of us, and cocked our head on one side, and said, 'Don't go! Don't go!'

The girl seemed alarmed. We began to get a little nervous ourselves, but we had begun it, and we meant to go through with it.

We said, 'Do you know, Jane (her name wasn't Jane, but that wasn't our fault), 'do you know, Jane, I think you're an uncommonly nice girl,' and we said, 'click,' and dug her in the ribs with our elbow, and then chucked her under the chin. The whole thing seemed to fall flat. There was nobody there to laugh or applaud. We wished we hadn't done it. It seemed stupid, when you came to think of it. We began to feel frightened. The business wasn't going as we expected; but we screwed up our courage, and went on.

We put on the customary expression of comic imbecility, and beckoned the girl to us. We have never seen this fail on the stage.

But this girl seemed made wrong. She got behind the sofa, and screamed 'Help!'

We have never known them to do this on the stage, and it threw us out in our plans. We did not know exactly what to do. We regretted that we had ever begun this job, and heartily wished ourselves out of it. But it appeared foolish to pause then, when we were more than halfway through, and we made a rush to get it over.

We chivied the girl round the sofa, and caught her near the door, and kissed her. She scratched our face, yelled police, murder, and fire, and fled from the room.

Our friend came in almost immediately. He said, 'I say, J., old man, are you drunk?'

We told him no, that we were only a student of the drama.

His wife then entered in a towering passion. She didn't ask us if we were drunk. She said, 'How dare you come here in this state!'

53

We endeavoured, unsuccessfully, to induce her to believe that we were sober; and we explained that our course of conduct was what was always pursued on the stage.

She said she didn't care what was done on the stage, it wasn't going to be pursued in her house; and that if her husband's friends couldn't behave as gentlemen they had better stop away.

A few more chatty remarks were exchanged, and then we took our leave.

The following morning we received a letter from a firm of solicitors in Lincoln's Inn with reference, so they put it, to the brutal and unprovoked assault committed by us on the previous afternoon upon the person of their client, Miss Matilda Hemmings. The letter stated that we had punched Miss Hemmings in the side, struck her under the chin, and, afterwards, seizing her as she was leaving the room, proceeded to commit a gross assault, into the particulars of which it was needless for them to enter at greater length.

It added that if we were prepared to render an ample written apology, and to pay fifty pounds compensation, they would advise their client, Miss Matilda Hemmings, to allow the matter to drop, otherwise, criminal proceedings would at once be commenced against us.

We took the letter to our own solicitors, and explained the circumstances to them. They said it seemed to be a very sad case, but advised us to pay the fifty pounds, and we borrowed the money, and did so.

Since then we have lost faith, somehow, in the British drama as a guide to the conduct of life.

The Woman of the Saeter

Wild reindeer stalking is hardly so exciting a sport as the evening's verandah talk in Norroway hotels would lead the trustful traveller to suppose. Under the charge of your guide, a very young man with the dreamy, wistful eyes of those who live in valleys, you leave the farmstead early in the forenoon, arriving towards twilight at the desolate hut which, for so long as you remain upon the uplands, will be your somewhat cheerless headquarters.

Next morning, in the chill, mist-laden dawn you rise; and, after a breakfast of coffee and dried fish, shoulder your Remington, and step forth silently into the raw, damp air; the guide locking the door behind you, the key grating harshly in the rusty lock.

For hour after hour you toil over the steep, stony ground, or wind through the pines, speaking in whispers, lest your voice reach the quick ears of your prey, that keeps its head ever pressed against the wind. Here and there, in the hollows of the hills, lie wide fields of snow, over which you pick your steps thoughtfully, listening to the smothered thunder of the torrent, tunnelling its way beneath your feet, and wondering whether the frozen arch above it be at all points as firm as is desirable. Now and again, as in single file you walk cautiously along some jagged ridge, you catch glimpses of the green world three thousand feet below you; though you gaze not long upon the view, for your attention is chiefly directed to watching the footprints of the guide, lest by deviating to the right or left you find yourself at one stride back in the valley—or, to be more correct, are found there.

These things you do, and as exercise they are healthful and invigorating. But a reindeer you never see, and unless, overcoming the prejudices of your British-bred conscience, you care to take an occasional pop at a fox, you had better have left your rifle at the hut, and, instead, have brought a stick, which would have been helpful. Notwithstanding which the guide continues sanguine, and in broken English, helped out by stirring gesture, tells of the terrible slaughter generally done by sportsmen under his superintendence, and of the vast herds that generally infest these fields; and when you grow sceptical upon the subject of Reins he whispers alluringly of Bears.

Once in a way you will come across a track, and will follow it breathlessly for hours, and it will lead to a sheer precipice. Whether the explanation is suicide, or a reprehensible tendency on the part of the animal towards practical joking, you are left to decide for yourself. Then, with many rough miles between you and your rest, you abandon the chase.

But I speak from personal experience merely.

All day long we had tramped through the pitiless rain, stopping only for an hour at noon to eat some dried venison, and smoke a pipe beneath the shelter of an overhanging cliff. Soon afterwards Michael knocked over a ryper (a bird that will hardly take the trouble to hop out of your way) with his gunbarrel, which incident cheered us a little, and, later on, our flagging spirits were still further revived by the discovery of apparently very recent deer tracks. These we followed, forgetful, in our eagerness, of the lengthening distance back to the hut, of the fading daylight, of the gathering mist. The track led us higher and higher, farther and farther into the mountains, until on the shores of a desolate rockbound vand it abruptly ended, and we stood staring at one another, and the snow began to fall.

Unless in the next half hour we could chance upon a saeter, this meant passing the night upon the mountain. Michael and I looked at the guide, but though, with characteristic Norwegian sturdiness, he put a bold face upon it, we could see that in that deepening darkness he knew no more than we did. Wasting no time on words, we made straight for the nearest point of descent, knowing that any human habitation must be far below us.

Down we scrambled, heedless of torn clothes and bleeding hands, the darkness pressing closer round us. Then suddenly it became black—black as pitch—and we could only hear each other. Another step might mean death. We stretched out our hands, and felt each other. Why we spoke in whispers, I do not know, but we seemed afraid of our own voices. We agreed there was nothing for it but to stop where we were till morning, clinging to the short grass; so we lay there side by side, for what may have been five minutes or may have been an hour. Then, attempting to turn, I lost my grip and rolled. I made convulsive efforts to clutch the ground, but the incline was too steep. How far I fell I could not say, but at last something stopped me. I felt it cautiously with my foot; it did not yield, so I twisted myself round and touched it with my hand. It seemed planted firmly in the earth. I passed my arm along to the right, then to the left. Then I shouted with joy. It was a fence.

Rising and groping about me, I found an opening, and passed through, and crept forward with palms outstretched until I touched the logs of a hut; then, feeling my way round, discovered the door, and knocked. There came no response, so I knocked louder; then pushed, and the heavy woodwork yielded, groaning. But the darkness within was even darker than the darkness without. The others had contrived to crawl down and join me. Michael struck a wax vesta and held it up, and slowly the room came out of the darkness and stood round us.

Then something rather startling happened. Giving one swift glance about him, our guide uttered a cry, and rushed out into the night, and disappeared. We followed to the door, and called after him, but only a voice came to us out of the blackness, and the only words that we could catch, shrieked back in terror, were: 'The woman of the saeter—the woman of the saeter.'

'Some foolish superstition about the place, I suppose,' said Michael. 'In these mountain solitudes men breed ghosts for company. Let us make a fire. Perhaps, when he sees the light, his desire for food and shelter may get the better of his fears.'

We felt about in the small enclosure round the house, and gathered juniper and birch twigs, and kindled a fire upon the open stove built in the corner of the room. Fortunately, we had some dried reindeer and bread in our bag, and on that and the ryper, and the contents of our flasks, we supped. Afterwards, to while away the time, we made an inspection of the strange eyrie we had lighted on.

It was an old log-built saeter. Some of these mountain farmsteads are as old as the stone ruins of other countries. Carvings of strange beasts and demons were upon its blackened rafters, and on the lintel, in runic letters, ran this legend: 'Hund built me in the days of Haarfager.' The house consisted of two large apartments. Originally, no doubt, these had been separate dwellings standing beside one another, but they were now connected by a long, low gallery. Most of the scanty furniture was almost as ancient as the walls themselves, but many articles of a comparatively recent date had been added. All was now, however, rotting and falling into decay.

The place appeared to have been deserted suddenly by its last occupants. Household utensils lay as they were left, rust and dirt encrusted on them.

An open book, limp and mildewed, lay face downwards on the table, while many others were scattered about both rooms, together with much paper, scored with faded ink. The curtains hung in shreds about the windows; a woman's cloak, of an antiquated fashion, drooped from a nail behind the door. In an oak chest we found a tumbled heap of yellow letters. They were of various dates, extending over a period of four months, and with them, apparently intended to receive them, lay a large envelope, inscribed with an address in London that has since disappeared.

Strong curiosity overcoming faint scruples, we read them by the dull glow of the burning juniper twigs, and, as we lay aside the last of them, there rose from the depths below us a wailing cry, and all night long it rose and died away, and rose again, and died away again; whether born of our brain or of some human thing, God knows.

And these, a little altered and shortened, are the letters:

Extract from first letter:

I cannot tell you, my dear Joyce, what a haven of peace this place is to me after the racket and fret of town. I am almost quite recovered already, and am growing stronger every day; and, joy of joys, my brain has come back to me, fresher and more vigorous, I think, for its holiday. In this silence and solitude my thoughts flow freely, and the difficulties of my task are disappearing as if by magic. We are perched upon a tiny plateau halfway up the mountain. On one side the rock rises almost perpendicularly, piercing the sky; while on the other, two thousand feet below us, the torrent hurls itself into black waters of the fiord. The house consists of two rooms—or, rather, it is two cabins connected by a passage. The larger one we use as a living room, and the other is our sleeping apartment. We have no servant, but do everything for ourselves. I fear sometimes Muriel must find it lonely. The nearest human habitation is eight miles away, across the mountain, and not a soul comes near us. I spend as much time as I can with her, however, during the day, and make up for it by working at night after she has gone to sleep, and when I question her, she only laughs, and answers that she loves to have me all to herself. (Here you will smile cynically, I know, and say, 'Humph, I wonder will she say the same when they have been married six years instead of six months.') At the rate I am working now I shall have finished my first volume by the end of August, and then, my dear fellow, you must try and come over, and we will walk and talk together 'amid these storm-reared temples of the gods.' I have felt a new man since I arrived here. Instead of having to 'cudgel my brains,' as we say, thoughts crowd upon me. This work will make my name.

Part of the third letter, the second being mere talk about the book
(a history apparently) that the man was writing:

My dear Joyce, I have written you two letters—this will make the third—but have been unable to post them. Every day I have been expecting a visit from some farmer or villager, for the Norwegians are kindly people towards strangers—to say nothing of the inducements of trade. A fortnight having passed, however, and the commissariat question having become serious, I yesterday set out before dawn, and made my way down to the valley; and this gives me something to tell you. Nearing the village, I met a peasant woman. To my intense surprise, instead of returning my salutation, she stared at me as if I were some wild animal, and shrank away from me as far as the width of the road would permit. In the village the same experience awaited me. The children ran from me, the people avoided me. At last a grey-haired old man appeared to take pity on me, and from him I learnt the explanation of the mystery. It seems there is a strange superstition attaching to this house in which we are living. My things were brought up here by the two men who accompanied me from Dronthiem, but the natives are afraid to go near the place, and prefer to keep as far as possible from anyone connected with it.

The story is that the house was built by one Hund, 'a maker of runes' (one of the old saga writers, no doubt), who lived here with his young wife. All went peacefully until, unfortunately for him, a certain maiden stationed at a neighbouring saeter grew to love him. Forgive me if I am telling you what you know, but a 'saeter' is the name given to the upland pastures to which, during the summer, are sent the cattle, generally under the charge of one or more of the maids. Here for three months these girls will live in their lonely huts entirely shut off from the world. Customs change little in this land. Two or three such stations are within climbing distance of this house, at this day, looked after by the farmers' daughters, as in the days of Hund, 'maker of runes.'

Every night, by devious mountain paths, the woman would come and tap lightly at Hund's door. Hund had built himself two cabins, one behind the other (these are now, as I think I have explained to you, connected by a passage); the smaller one was the homestead, in the other he carved and wrote, so that while the young wife slept the 'maker of runes' and the saeter woman sat whispering.

One night, however, the wife learnt all things, but said no word. Then, as now, the ravine in front of the enclosure was crossed by a slight bridge of planks, and over this bridge the woman of the saeter passed and repassed each night. On a day when Hund had gone down to fish in the fiord, the wife took an axe, and hacked and hewed at the bridge, yet it still looked firm and solid; and that night, as Hund sat waiting in his workshop, there struck upon his ears a piercing cry, and a crashing of logs and rolling rock, and then again the dull roaring of the torrent far below.

But the woman did not die unavenged, for that winter a man, skating far down the fiord, noticed a curious object embedded in the ice; and when, stooping, he looked closer, he saw two corpses, one gripping the other by the throat, and the bodies were the bodies of Hund and his young wife.

Since then, they say the woman of the saeter haunts Hund's house, and if she sees a light within she taps upon the door, and no man may keep her out. Many, at different times, have tried to occupy the house, but strange tales are told of them. 'Men do not live at Hund's saeter,' said my old grey-haired friend, concluding his tale, 'they die there.' I have persuaded some of the braver of the villagers to bring what provisions and other necessaries we require up to a plateau about a mile from the house and leave them there. That is the most I have been able to do. It comes somewhat as a shock to one to find men and women—fairly educated and intelligent as many of them are—slaves to fears that one would expect a child to laugh at. But there is no reasoning with superstition.

Extract from the same letter, but from a part seemingly written a day or two later:

At home I should have forgotten such a tale an hour after I had heard it, but these mountain vastnesses seem strangely fit to be the last stronghold of the supernatural. The woman haunts me already. At night, instead of working, I find myself listening for her tapping at the door; and yesterday an incident occurred that makes me fear for my own common sense. I had gone out for a long walk alone, and the twilight was thickening into darkness as I neared home. Suddenly looking up from my reverie, I saw, standing on a knoll the other side of the ravine, the figure of a woman. She held a cloak about her head, and I could not see her face. I took off my cap, and called out a goodnight to her, but she never moved or spoke. Then, God knows why, for my brain was full of other thoughts at the time, a clammy chill crept over me, and my tongue grew dry and parched. I stood rooted to the spot, staring at her across the yawning gorge that divided us, and slowly she moved away, and passed into the gloom; and I continued my way. I have said nothing to Muriel, and shall not. The effect the story has had upon myself warns me not to.

From a letter dated eleven days later:

She has come. I have known she would since that evening I saw her on the mountain, and last night she came, and we have sat and looked into each other's eyes. You will say, of course, that I am mad—that I have not recovered from my fever—that I have been working too hard—that I have heard a foolish tale, and that it has filled my overstrung brain with foolish fancies—I have told myself all that. But the thing came, nevertheless—a creature of flesh and blood? a creature of air? a creature of my own imagination? what matter; it was real to me.

It came last night, as I sat working, alone. Each night I have waited for it, listened for it—longed for it, I know now. I heard the passing of its feet upon the bridge, the tapping of its hand upon the door, three times—tap, tap, tap. I felt my loins grow cold, and a pricking pain about my head, and I gripped my chair with both hands, and waited, and again there came the tapping—tap, tap, tap. I rose and slipped the bolt of the door leading to the other room, and again I waited, and again there came the tapping—tap, tap, tap. Then I opened the heavy outer door, and the wind rushed past me, scattering my papers, and the woman entered in, and I closed the door behind her. She threw her hood back from her head, and unwound a kerchief from about her neck, and laid it on the table. Then she crossed and sat before the fire, and I noticed her bare feet were damp with the night dew.

I stood over against her and gazed at her, and she smiled at me—a strange, wicked smile, but I could have laid my soul at her feet. She never spoke or moved, and neither did I feel the need of spoken words, for I understood the meaning of those upon the Mount when they said, 'Let us make here tabernacles: it is good for us to be here.'

How long a time passed thus I do not know, but suddenly the woman held her hand up, listening, and there came a faint sound from the other room. Then swiftly she drew her hood about her face and passed out, closing the door softly behind her; and I drew back the bolt of the inner door and waited, and hearing nothing more, sat down, and must have fallen asleep in my chair.

I awoke, and instantly there flashed through my mind the thought of the kerchief the woman had left behind her, and I started from my chair to hide it. But the table was already laid for breakfast, and my wife sat with her elbows on the table and her head between her hands, watching me with a look in her eyes that was new to me.

She kissed me, though her lips were a little cold, and I argued to myself that the whole thing must have been a dream. But later in the day, passing the open door when her back was towards me, I saw her take the kerchief from a locked chest and look at it.

I have told myself it must have been a kerchief of her own, and that all the rest has been my imagination—that if not, then my strange visitant was no spirit, but a woman, and that, if human thing knows human thing, it was no creature of flesh and blood that sat beside me last night. Besides, what woman would she be? The nearest saeter is a three hours' climb to a strong man, the paths are dangerous even in daylight: what woman would have found them in the night? What woman would have chilled the air around her, and have made the blood flow cold through all my veins? Yet if she come again I will speak to her. I will stretch out my hand and see whether she be mortal thing or only air.

The fifth letter:

My dear Joyce, Whether your eyes will ever see these letters is doubtful. From this place I shall never send them. They would read to you as the ravings of a madman. If ever I return to England I may one day show them to you, but when I do it will be when I, with you, can laugh over them. At present I write them merely to hide away—putting the words down on paper saves my screaming them aloud.

She comes each night now, taking the same seat beside the embers, and fixing upon me those eyes, with the hell-light in them, that burn into my brain; and at rare times she smiles, and all my being passes out of me, and is hers. I make no attempt to work. I sit listening for her footsteps on the creaking bridge, for the rustling of her feet upon the grass, for the tapping of her hand upon the door. No word is uttered between us. Each day I say: 'When she comes tonight I will speak to her. I will stretch out my hand and touch her.' Yet when she enters, all thought and will goes out from me.

Last night, as I stood gazing at her, my soul filled with her wondrous beauty as a lake with moonlight, her lips parted, and she started from her chair, and, turning, I thought I saw a white face pressed against the window, but as I looked it vanished. Then she drew her cloak about her, and passed out. I slid back the bolt I always draw now, and stole into the other room, and, taking down the lantern, held it above the bed. But Muriel's eyes were closed as if in sleep.

Extract from the sixth letter.

It is not the night I fear, but the day. I hate the sight of this woman with whom I live, whom I call 'wife'. I shrink from the blow of her cold lips, the curse of her stony eyes. She has seen, she has learnt; I feel it, I know it. Yet she winds her arms around my neck, and calls me sweetheart, and smooths my hair with her soft, false hands. We speak mocking words of love to one another, but I know her cruel eyes are ever following me. She is plotting her revenge, and I hate her, I hate her, I hate her!

Part of the seventh letter:

This morning I went down to the fiord. I told her I should not be back until the evening. She stood by the door watching me until we were mere specks to one another, and a promontory of the mountain shut me from view. Then, turning aside from the track, I made my way, running and stumbling over the jagged ground, round to the other side of the mountain, and began to climb again. It was slow, weary work. Often I had to go miles out of my road to avoid a ravine, and twice I reached a high point only to have to descend again. But at length I crossed the ridge, and crept down to a spot from where, concealed, I could spy upon my own house. She—my wife—stood by the flimsy bridge. A short hatchet, such as butchers use, was in her hand. She leant against a pine trunk, with her arm behind her, as one stands whose back aches with long stooping in some cramped position; and even at that distance I could see the cruel smile about her lips.

Then I recrossed the ridge, and crawled down again, and, waiting until evening, walked slowly up the path. As I came in view of the house she saw me, and waved her handkerchief to me, and, in answer, I waved my hat, and shouted curses at her that the wind whirled away into the torrent. She met me with a kiss, and I breathed no hint to her that I had seen. Let her devil's work remain undisturbed. Let it prove to me what manner of thing this is that haunts me. If it be a spirit, then the bridge will bear it safely: if it be woman—

But I dismiss the thought. If it be human thing why does it sit gazing at me, never speaking; why does my tongue refuse to question it; why does all power forsake me in its presence, so that I stand as in a dream? Yet if it be spirit, why do I hear the passing of her feet; and why does the night rain glisten on her hair?

I force myself back into my chair. It is far into the night, and I am alone, waiting, listening. If it be spirit, she will come to me; and if it be woman, I shall hear her cry above the storm—unless it be a demon mocking me.

I have heard the cry. It rose, piercing and shrill, above the storm, above the riving and rending of the bridge, above the downward crashing of the logs and loosened stones. I hear it as I listen now. It is cleaving its way upward from the depths below. It is wailing through the room as I sit writing.

I have crawled upon my belly to the utmost edge of the still standing pier until I could feel with my hand the jagged splinters left by the fallen planks, and have looked down. But the chasm was full to the brim with darkness. I shouted, but the wind shook my voice into mocking laughter. I sit here, feebly striking at the madness that is creeping nearer and nearer to me. I tell myself the whole thing is but the fever in my brain. The bridge was rotten. The storm was strong. The cry is but a single one among the many voices of the mountain. Yet still I listen, and it rises, clear and shrill, above the moaning of the pines, above the mighty sobbing of the waters. It beats like blows upon my skull, and I know that she will never come again.

Extract from the last letter:

I shall address an envelope to you, and leave it among them. Then, should I never come back, some chance wanderer may one day find and post them to you, and you will know.

My books and writings remain untouched. We sit together of a night— this woman I call 'wife' and I—she holding in her hands some knitted thing that never grows longer by a single stitch, and I with a volume before me that is ever open at the same page. And day and night we watch each other stealthily, moving to and fro about the silent house; and at times, looking round swiftly, I catch the smile upon her lips before she has time to smooth it away.

We speak like strangers about this and that, making talk to hide our thoughts. We make a pretence of busying ourselves about whatever will help us to keep apart from one another.

At night, sitting here between the shadows and the dull glow of the smouldering twigs, I sometimes think I hear the tapping I have learnt to listen for, and I start from my seat, and softly open the door and look out. But only the night stands there. Then I close to the latch, and she—the living woman—asks me in her purring voice what sound I heard, hiding a smile as she stoops low over her work, and I answer lightly, and, moving towards her, put my arm about her, feeling her softness and her suppleness, and wondering, supposing I held her close to me with one arm while pressing her from me with the other, how long before I should hear the cracking of her bones.

For here, amid these savage solitudes, I also am grown savage. The old primeval passions of love and hate stir within me, and they are fierce and cruel and strong, beyond what you men of the later ages could understand. The culture of the centuries has fallen from me as a flimsy garment whirled away by the mountain wind; the old savage instincts of the race lie bare. One day I shall twine my fingers about her full white throat, and her eyes will slowly come towards me, and her lips will part, and the red tongue creep out; and backwards, step by step, I shall push her before me, gazing the while upon her bloodless face, and it will be my turn to smile. Backwards through the open door, backwards along the garden path between the juniper bushes, backwards till her heels are overhanging the ravine, and she grips life with nothing but her little toes, I shall force her, step by step, before me. Then I shall lean forward, closer, closer, till I kiss her purpling lips, and down, down, down, past the startled seabirds, past the white spray of the foss, past the downward peeping pines, down, down, down, we will go together, till we find my love where she lies sleeping beneath the waters of the fiord.

With these words ended the last letter, unsigned. At the first streak of dawn we left the house, and, after much wandering, found our way back to the valley. But of our guide we heard no news. Whether he remained still upon the mountain, or whether by some false step he had perished upon that night, we never learnt.

The Ghost of the Marchioness
of Appleford

This is the story, among others, of Henry the waiter—or, as he now prefers to call himself, Henri—told to me in the long dining room of the Riffel Alp Hotel, where I once stayed for a melancholy week 'between seasons,' sharing the echoing emptiness of the place with two maiden ladies, who talked all day to one another in frightened whispers. Henry's construction I have discarded for its amateurishness; his method being generally to commence a story at the end, and then, working backwards to the beginning, wind up with the middle. But in all other respects I have endeavoured to retain his method, which was individual; and this, I think, is the story as he would have told it to me himself, had he told it in this order.

My first place—well to be honest, it was a coffee shop in the Mile End Road—I'm not ashamed of it. We all have our beginnings. Young Kipper, as we called him—he had no name of his own, not that he knew of anyhow, and that seemed to fit him down to the ground—had 'fixed his pitch just outside, between our door and the music hall at the corner; and sometimes, when I might happen to have a bit on, I'd get a paper from him, and pay him for it, when the governor was not about, with a mug of coffee, and odds and ends that the other customers had left on their plates—an arrangement that suited both of us. He was just about as sharp as they make boys, even in the Mile End Road, which is saying a good deal; and now and then, spying around among the right sort, and keeping his ears open, he would put me up to a good thing, and I would tip him a bob or a tanner as the case might be. He was the sort that gets on—you know.

One day in he walks, for all the world as if the show belonged to him, with a young imp of a girl on his arm, and down they sits at one of the tables.

'Garsong,' he calls out, 'what's the menoo today?'

'The menoo today,' I says, 'is that you get outside 'fore I clip you over the ear, and that you take that back and put it where you found it,' meaning o' course, the kid.

She was a pretty little thing, even then, in spite of the dirt, with those eyes like saucers and red hair. It used to be called 'carrots' in those days. Now all the swells have taken it up—or as near as they can get to it—and it's auburn.

''Enery,' he replied to me, without so much as turning a hair, 'I'm afraid you're forgetting your position. When I'm on the kerb shouting "Speshul!" and you comes to me with yer 'a'penny in yer 'and, you're master an' I'm man. When I comes into your shop to order refreshments, and to pay for 'em, I'm boss, Savvy? You can bring me a rasher and two eggs, and see that they're this season's. The lidy will have a full-sized haddick and a cocoa.'

Well, there was justice in what he said. He always did have sense, and I took his order. You don't often see anybody put it away like that girl did. I took it she hadn't had a square meal for many a long day. She polished off a ninepenny haddick, skin and all, and after that she had two penny rashers, with six slices of bread and butter—'doorsteps,' as we used to call them— and two half pints of cocoa, which is a meal in itself the way we used to make it. Kipper must have had a bit of luck that day. He couldn't have urged her on more had it been a free feed.

''Ave an egg,' he suggested, the moment the rashers had disappeared. 'One of these eggs will just about finish yer.'

'I don't really think as I can,' says she, after considering like.

'Well, you know your own strength,' he answers. 'Perhaps you're best without it. Speshully if yer not used to 'igh living.'

I was glad to see them finish, 'cause I was beginning to get a bit nervous about the coin, but he paid up right enough, and give me a ha'penny for myself

That was the first time I ever waited upon those two, but it wasn't to be the last by many a long chalk, as you'll see. He often used to bring her in after that. Who she was and what she was he didn't know, and she didn't know, so there was a pair of them. She'd run away from an old woman down Limehouse way, who used to beat her. That was all she could tell him. He got her a lodging with an old woman, who had an attic in the same house where he slept—when it would run to that—taught her to yell 'Speshul!' and found a corner for her. There ain't room for boys and girls in the Mile End Road. They're either kids down there or they're grown-ups. Kipper and Carrots—as we named her—looked upon themselves as sweethearts, though he couldn't have been more than fifteen, and she barely twelve; and that he was regular gone on her anyone could see with half an eye. Not that he was soft about it—that wasn't his style. He kept her in order, and she had just to mind, which I guess was a good thing for her, and when she wanted it he'd use his hand on her, and make no bones about it. That's the way among that class. They up and give the old woman a friendly clump, just as you or me would swear at the missus, or fling a boot jack at her. They don't mean anything more.

I left the coffee shop later on for a place in the City, and saw nothing more of them for five years. When I did it was at a restaurant in Oxford Street—one of those amatoor shows run by a lot of women, who know nothing about the business, and spend the whole day gossiping and flirting—'loveshops,' I call 'em. There was a yellow-haired lady manageress who never heard you when you spoke to her, 'cause she was always trying to hear what some seedy old fool would be whispering to her across the counter. Then there were waitresses, and their notion of waiting was to spend an hour talking to a twopenny cup of coffee, and to look haughty and insulted whenever anybody as really wanted something ventured to ask for it. A frizzle-haired cashier used to make love all day out of her pigeonhole with the two box-office boys from the Oxford Music Hall, who took it turn and turn about. Sometimes she'd leave off to take a customer's money, and sometimes she wouldn't. I've been to some rummy places in my time; and a waiter ain't the blind owl as he's supposed to be. But never in my life have I seen so much love-making, not all at once, as used to go on in that place. It was a dismal, gloomy sort of hole, and spoony couples seemed to scent it out by instinct, and would spend hours there over a pot of tea and assorted pastry. 'Idyllic,' some folks would have thought it: I used to get the fair dismals watching it. There was one girl—a weird-looking creature with red eyes and long thin hands, that gave you the creeps to look at. She'd come in regular with her young man, a pale-faced nervous sort of chap, at three o'clock every afternoon. Theirs was the funniest love-making I ever saw. She'd pinch him under the table, and run pins into him, and he'd sit with his eyes glued on her as if she'd been a steaming dish of steak and onions and he a starving beggar the other side of the window. A strange story that was—as I came to learn it later on. I'll tell you that, one day.

I'd been engaged for the 'heavy work,' but as the heaviest order I ever heard given there was for a cold ham and chicken, which I had to slip out for to the nearest cookshop, I must have been chiefly useful from an orna-mental point of view.

I'd been there about a fortnight, and was feeling pretty sick of it, when in walked young Kipper. I didn't know him at first, he'd changed so. He was swinging a silver-mounted crutch stick, which was the kind that was fashionable just then, and was dressed in a showy check suit and a white hat. But the thing that struck me most was his gloves. I suppose I hadn't improved quite so much myself, for he knew me in a moment, and held out his hand.

'What, 'Enery!' he says. 'You've moved on, then!'

'Yes,' I says, shaking hands with him, 'and I could move on again from this shop without feeling sad. But you've got on a bit?' I says.

'So-so,' he says, 'I'm a journalist.'

'Oh,' I says, 'what sort?' for I'd seen a good many of that lot during six months I'd spent at a house in Fleet Street, and their get-up hadn't sumptu-ousness about it, so to speak. Kipper's rigout must have totted up to a tidy little sum. He had a diamond pin in his tie that must have cost somebody fifty quid, if not him.

'Well,' he answers, 'I don't wind out the confidential advice to old Beaky, and that sort of thing. I do the tips, yer know. "Cap'n Kit," that's my name.'

'What, *the* Captain Kit?' I says. O' course I'd heard of him.

'Be 'old!' he says.

'Oh, it's easy enough,' he goes on. 'Some of 'em's bound to come out right, and when one does, you take it from me, our paper mentions the fact. And when it is a wrong 'un—well, a man can't always be shouting about himself, can 'e?'

He ordered a cup of coffee. He said he was waiting for someone, and we got to chatting about old times. 'How's Carrots?' I asked.

'Miss Caroline Trevelyan,' he answered, 'is doing well.'

'Oh,' I says, 'you've found out her fam'ly name, then?'

'We've found out one or two things about that lidy,' he replies. 'D'yer remember 'er dancing?'

'I have seen her flinging her petticoats about outside the shop, when the copper wasn't by, if that's what you mean,' I says.

'That's what I mean,' he answers. 'That's all the rage now, "skirt-dancing" they calls it. She's a-coming out at the Oxford tomorrow. It's 'er I'm waiting for. She's a-coming on, I tell you she is,' he says.

'Shouldn't wonder,' says I. 'That was her disposition.'

'And there's another thing we've found out about 'er,' he says. He leant over the table, and whispered it, as if he was afraid that anybody else might hear: 'She's got a voice.'

'Yes,' I says, 'some women have.'

'Ah,' he says, 'but 'er voice is the sort of voice yer want to listen to.'

'Oh,' I says, 'that's its speciality, is it?'

'That's it, sonny,' he replied.

She came in a little later. I'd a' known her anywhere for her eyes, and her red hair, in spite of her being that clean you might have eaten your dinner out of her hand. And as for her clothes! Well, I've mixed a good deal with the toffs in my time, and I've seen duchesses dressed more showily and maybe more expensively, but her clothes seemed to be just a framework to show her up. She was a beauty, you can take it from me; and it's not to be wondered that the La-De-Das were round her when they did see her, like flies round an open jam tart.

Before three months were up she was the rage of London—leastways of the music-hall part of it—with her portrait in all the shop windows, and interviews with her in half the newspapers. It seems she was the daughter of an officer who had died in India when she was a baby, and the niece of a bishop somewhere in Australia. He was dead too. There didn't seem to be any of her ancestry as wasn't dead, but they had all been swells. She had been educated privately, she had, by a relative; and had early displayed an aptitude for dancing, though her friends at first had much opposed her going upon the stage. There was a lot more of it—you know the sort of thing. Of course, she was a connection of one of our best-known judges—they all are—and she merely acted in order to support a grandmother, or an invalid sister, I forget which. A wonderful talent for swallowing, these newspaper chaps has, some of 'em!

Kipper never touched a penny of her money, but if he had been her agent at 25 per cent he couldn't have worked harder, and he just kept up the hum about her, till if you didn't want to hear anything more about Caroline Trevelyan, your only chance would have been to lie in bed and never look at a newspaper. It was Caroline Trevelyan at Home, Caroline Trevelyan at Brighton, Caroline Trevelyan and the Shah of Persia, Caroline Trevelyan and the Old Apple-woman. When it wasn't Caroline Trevelyan herself it would be Caroline Trevelyan's dog as would be doing something out of the common, getting himself lost or summoned or drowned—it didn't matter much what.

I moved from Oxford Street to the new Horse-shoe that year—it had just been rebuilt—and there I saw a good deal of them, for they came in to lunch there or supper pretty regular. Young Kipper—or the 'Captain' as everybody called him—gave out that he was her half-brother.

'I 'ad to be some sort of a relation, you see,' he explained to me. 'I'd a' been 'er brother out and out; that would have been simpler, only the family likeness wasn't strong enough. Our styles o' beauty ain't similar.' They certainly wasn't.

'Why don't you marry her,' I says, 'and have done with it?'

He looked thoughtful at that. 'I did think of it,' he says, 'and I know, jolly well, that if I 'ad suggested it 'fore she'd found herself, she'd have agreed, but don't seem quite fair now.'

'How d'ye mean fair?' I says.

'Well, not fair to 'er,' he says. 'I've got on all right, in a small way; but she—well, she can just 'ave 'er pick of the nobs. There's one on 'em as I've made inquiries about. 'E'll be a dook, if a kid pegs out as is expected to, and anyhow 'e'll be a markis, and 'e means the straight thing—no errer. It ain't fair for me to stand in 'er way.'

'Well,' I says, 'you know your own business, but it seems to me she wouldn't have much way to stand in if it hadn't been for you.'

'Oh, that's all right,' he says. 'I'm fond enough of the gell, but I shan't clamour for a tombstone with wiolets, even if she ain't ever Mrs Capt'n Kit. Business is business; and I ain't going to queer 'er pitch for 'er.'

I've often wondered what she'd a' said, if he'd up and put the case to her plain, for she was a good sort; but, naturally enough, her head was a bit swelled, and she'd read so much rot about herself in the papers that she'd got at last to half believe some of it. The thought of her connection with the well-known judge seemed to hamper her at times, and she wasn't quite so chummy with Kipper as used to be the case in the Mile End Road days, and he wasn't the sort as is slow to see a thing.

One day when he was having lunch by himself, and I was waiting on him, he says, raising his glass to his lips, 'Well, 'Enery, here's luck to yer! I won't be seeing you agen for some time.'

'Oh,' I says, 'and what about—'

'That's all right,' he interrupts. 'I've fixed up that—a treat. Truth, that's why I'm going.'

I thought at first he meant she was going with him.

'No,' he says, 'she's going to be the Duchess of Ridingshire with the kind consent o' the kid I spoke about. If not, she'll be the Marchioness of Appleford. 'E's doing the square thing. There's going to be a quiet marriage tomorrow at the register office, and then I'm off.'

'What need for you to go?' I says.

'No need,' he says, 'it's a fancy o' mine. You see, me gone, there's nothing to 'amper 'er—nothing to interfere with 'er settling down as a quiet, respectable toff. With a 'alf-brother, who's always got to be spry with some fake about 'is lineage and 'is ancestral estates, and who drops 'is 'h's,' complications are sooner or later bound to a-rise. Me out of it—everything's simple. Savvy?'

Well, that's just how it happened. Of course, there was a big row when the family heard of it, and a smart lawyer was put up to try and undo the thing. No expense was spared, you bet; but it was all no go. Nothing could be found out against her. She just sat tight and said nothing. So the thing had to stand. They went and lived quietly in the country and abroad for a year or two, and then folks forgot a bit, and they came back to London. I often used to see her name in print, and then the papers always said as how she was charming and graceful and beautiful, so I suppose the family had made up its mind to get used to her.

One evening in she comes to the Savoy. My wife put me up to getting that job, and a good job it is, mind you, when you know your way about. I'd never have had the cheek to try for it, if it hadn't been for the missis. She's a clever one—she is. I did a good day's work when I married her.

'You shave off that moustache of yours—it ain't an ornament,' she says to me, 'and chance it. Don't get attempting the lingo. Keep to the broken English, and put in a shrug or two. You can manage that all right.'

I followed her tip. Of course the manager saw through me, but I got in a 'Oui, monsieur' now and again, and they, being short-handed at the time, could not afford to be strict, I suppose. Anyhow, I got took on, and there I stopped for the whole season, and that was the making of me.

Well, as I was saying, in she comes to the supper rooms, and toffy enough she looked in her diamonds and furs, and as for haughtiness there wasn't a born marchioness she couldn't have given points to. She comes straight up to my table and sits down. Her husband was with her, but he didn't seem to have much to say, except to repeat her orders. Of course, I looked as if I'd never set eyes on her before in all my life, though all the time she was a-pecking at the mayonnaise and a-sipping at the Giessler, I was thinking of the coffee shop and of the ninepenny haddick and the pint of cocoa.

'Go and fetch my cloak,' she says to him after a while. 'I am cold.'

And up he gets and goes out.

She never moved her head, and spoke as though she was merely giving me some order, and I stands behind her chair, respectful like, and answers according to the same tip.

'Ever hear from Kipper?' she says to me.

'I have had one or two letters from him, your ladyship,' I answers.

'Oh, stow that,' she says. 'I am sick of "your ladyship." Talk English; I don't hear much of it. How's he getting on?'

'Seems to be doing himself well,' I says. 'He's started a hotel, and is regular raking it in, he tells me.'

'Wish I was behind the bar with him!' says she.

'Why, don't it work then?' I asks.

'It's just like a funeral with the corpse left out,' says she. 'Serves me jolly well right for being a fool!'

The Marquis, he comes back with her cloak at that moment, and I says: 'Certainement, madame,' and gets clear.

I often used to see her there, and when a chance occurred she would talk to me. It seemed to be a relief to her to use her own tongue, but it made me nervous at times for fear someone would hear her.

Then one day I got a letter from Kipper to say he was over for a holiday and was stopping at Morley's, and asking me to look him up.

He had not changed much except to get a bit fatter and more prosperous-looking. Of course, we talked about her ladyship, and I told him what she said.

'Rum things, women,' he says. 'Never know their own minds.'

'Oh, they know them all right when they get there,' I says. 'How could she tell what being a marchioness was like till she'd tried it?'

'Pity,' he says, musing like. 'I reckoned it the very thing she'd tumble to. I only came over to get a sight of 'er, and to satisfy myself as she was getting along all right. Seems I'd better a' stopped away.'

'You ain't ever thought of marrying yourself?' I asks.

'Yes, I have,' he says. 'It's slow for a man over thirty with no wife and kids to bustle him, you take it from me, and I ain't the talent for the Don Juan fake.'

'You're like me,' I says, 'a day's work, and then a pipe by your own fireside with your slippers on. That's my swarry. You'll find someone as will suit you before long.'

'No, I shan't,' says he. 'I've come across a few as might, if it 'adn't been for 'er. It's like the toffs as come out our way. They've been brought up on "ris de veau à la financier," and sich like, and it just spoils 'em for the bacon and greens.'

I give her the office the next time I see her, and they met accidental like in Kensington Gardens early one morning. What they said to one another I don't know, for he sailed that same evening, and, it being the end of the season, I didn't see her ladyship again for a long while.

When I did it was at the Hotel Bristol in Paris, and she was in widow's weeds, the Marquis having died eight months before. He never dropped into that dukedom, the kid turning out healthier than was expected, and hanging on; so she was still only a marchioness, and her fortune, though tidy, was nothing very big—not as that class reckons. By luck I was told off to wait on her, she having asked for someone as could speak English. She seemed glad to see me and to talk to me.

'Well,' I says, 'I suppose you'll be bossing that bar in Cape Town now before long?'

'Talk sense,' she answers. 'How can the Marchioness of Appleford marry a hotel keeper?'

'Why not,' I says, 'if she fancies him? What's the good of being a marchioness if you can't do what you like?'

'That's just it,' she snaps out. 'You can't. It would not be doing the straight thing by the family. No,' she says, 'I've spent their money, and I'm spending it now. They don't love me, but they shan't say as I have disgraced them. They've got their feelings—same as I've got mine.'

'Why not chuck the money?' I says. 'They'll be glad enough to get it back,' they being a poor lot, as I heard her say.

'How can I?' she says. 'It's a life interest. As long as I live I've got to have it, and as long as I live I've got to remain the Marchioness of Appleford.'

She finishes her soup, and pushes the plate away from her. 'As long as I live,' she says, talking to herself. 'By Jove!' she says, starting up. 'Why not?'

'Why not what?' I says.

'Nothing,' she answers. 'Get me an African telegraph form, and be quick about it!'

I fetched it for her, and she wrote it and gave it to the porter then and there; and, that done, she sat down and finished her dinner.

She was a bit short with me after that; so I judged it best to keep my own place.

In the morning she got an answer that seemed to excite her, and that afternoon she left; and the next I heard of her was a paragraph in the newspaper, headed—'Death of the Marchioness of Appleford. Sad accident.' It seemed she had gone for a row on one of the Italian lakes with no one but a boatman. A squall had come on, and the boat had capsized. The boatman had swum ashore, but he had been unable to save his passenger, and her body had never been recovered. The paper reminded its readers that she had formerly been the celebrated tragic actress, Caroline Trevelyan, daughter of the well-known Indian judge of that name.

It gave me the blues for a day or two—that bit of news. I had known her from a baby as you might say, and had taken an interest in her. You can call it silly, but hotels and restaurants seemed to me less interesting now there was no chance of ever seeing her come into one again.

I went from Paris to one of the smaller hotels in Venice. The missis thought I'd do well to pick up a bit of Italian, and perhaps she fancied Venice for herself. That's one of the advantages of our profession. You can go about. It was a second-rate sort of place, and one evening, just before light-ing-up time, I had the salle-à-manger all to myself, and had just taken up a paper when I hears the door open, and I turns round.

I saw 'her' coming down the room. There was no mistaking her. She wasn't that sort.

I sat with my eyes coming out of my head till she was close to me, and then I says:

'Carrots!' I says, in a whisper like. That was the name that come to me.

'Carrots it is,' she says, and down she sits just opposite to me, and then she laughs.

I could not speak, I could not move, I was that took aback, and the more frightened I looked the more she laughed till Kipper comes into the room. There was nothing ghostly about him. I never see a man look more as if he had backed the winner.

'Why, it's 'Enery,' he says, and he gives me a slap on the back as knocks the life into me again.

'I heard you was dead,' I says, still staring at her. 'I read it in the paper—"Death of the Marchioness of Appleford."'

'That's all right,' she says. 'The Marchioness of Appleford is as dead as a doornail, and a good job too. Mrs Captain Kit's my name, *née* Carrots.'

'You said as 'ow I'd find someone to suit me 'fore long,' says Kipper to me, 'and, by Jove! you were right; I 'ave. I was waiting till I found something equal to her ladyship, and I'd 'ave 'ad to wait a long time, I'm thinking, if I 'adn't come across this one 'ere,' and he tucks her up under his arm just as I remember his doing that day he first brought her into the coffee shop, and Lord, what a long time ago that was!

That is the story, among others, told me by Henry, the waiter. I have, at his request, substituted artificial names for real ones. For Henry tells me that at Cape Town Captain Kit's First-class Family and Commercial Hotel still runs, and that the landlady is still a beautiful woman with fine eyes and red hair, who might almost be taken for a duchess—until she opens her mouth, when her accent is found to be still slightly reminiscent of the Mile End Road.

The Passing of the
Third Floor Back

The neighbourhood of Bloomsbury Square towards four o'clock of a November afternoon is not so crowded as to secure to the stranger, of appearance anything out of the common, immunity from observation. Tibb's boy, screaming at the top of his voice that *she* was his honey, stopped suddenly, stepped backwards onto the toes of a voluble young lady wheeling a perambulator, remained deaf, apparently, to the somewhat personal remarks of the voluble young lady. Not until he had reached the next corner—and then more as a soliloquy than as information to the street—did Tibb's boy recover sufficient interest in his own affairs to remark that *he* was her bee. The voluble young lady herself, following some half a dozen yards behind, forgot her wrongs in contemplation of the stranger's back. There was this that was peculiar about the stranger's back: that instead of being flat it presented a decided curve. 'It ain't a 'ump, and it don't look like kervitcher of the spine,' observed the voluble young lady to herself. 'Blimy, if I don't believe 'e's taking 'ome 'is washing up his back.'

The constable at the corner, trying to seem busy doing nothing, noticed the stranger's approach with gathering interest. 'That's an odd sort of a walk of yours young man,' thought the constable. 'You take care you don't fall down and tumble over yourself.'

'Thought he was a young man,' murmured the constable, the stranger having passed him. 'He had a young face right enough.'

The daylight was fading. The stranger, finding it impossible to read the name of the street upon the corner house, turned back.

'Why 'tis a young man,' the constable told himself, 'a mere boy.'

'I beg your pardon,' said the stranger, 'but would you mind telling me my way to Bloomsbury Square.'

'This is Bloomsbury Square,' explained the constable. 'Leastways round the corner is. What number might you be wanting?'

The stranger took from the ticket pocket of his tightly buttoned overcoat a piece of paper, unfolded it and read it out: 'Mrs Pennycherry. Number Forty-eight.'

'Round to the left,' instructed him the constable, 'fourth house. Been recommended there?'

'By—by a friend,' replied the stranger. 'Thank you very much.'

'Ah,' muttered the constable to himself, 'guess you won't be calling him that by the end of the week, young—

'Funny,' added the constable, gazing after the retreating figure of the stranger. 'Seen plenty of the other sex as looked young behind and old in front. This cove looks young in front and old behind. Guess he'll look old all round if he stops long at Mother Pennycherry's: stingy old-cat.'

Constables whose beat included Bloomsbury Square had their reasons for not liking Mrs Pennycherry. Indeed, it might have been difficult to discover any human being with reasons for liking that sharp-featured lady. Maybe the keeping of second-rate boarding houses in the neighbourhood of Bloomsbury does not tend to develop the virtues of generosity and amiability.

Meanwhile the stranger, proceeding upon his way, had rung the bell of Number Forty-eight. Mrs Pennycherry, peeping from the area and catching a glimpse, above the railings, of a handsome if somewhat effeminate masculine face, hastened to readjust her widow's cap before the looking glass while directing Mary Jane to show the stranger, should he prove a problematical boarder, into the dining room, and to light the gas.

'And don't stop gossiping, and don't you take it upon yourself to answer questions. Say I'll be up in a minute,' were Mrs Pennycherry's further instructions, 'and mind you hide your hands as much as you can.'

'What are you grinning at?' demanded Mrs Pennycherry a couple of minutes later of the dingy Mary Jane.

'Wasn't grinning,' explained the meek Mary Jane, 'was only smiling to myself.'

'What at?'

'Dunno,' admitted Mary Jane. But still she went on smiling.

'What's he like then?' demanded Mrs Pennycherry. ''E ain't the usual sort,' was Mary Jane's opinion.

'Thank God for that,' ejaculated Mrs Pennycherry piously. 'Says 'e's been recommended, by a friend.'

'By whom?'

'By a friend. 'E didn't say no name.'

Mrs Pennycherry pondered. 'He's not the funny sort, is he?'

Not that sort at all. Mary Jane was sure of it.

Mrs Pennycherry ascended the stairs still pondering. As she entered the room the stranger rose and bowed. Nothing could have been simpler than the stranger's bow, yet there came with it to Mrs Pennycherry a rush of odd sensations long forgotten. For one brief moment Mrs Pennycherry saw herself an amiable well-bred lady, widow of a solicitor: a visitor had called to see her. It was but a momentary fancy. The next instant reality reasserted itself. Mrs Pennycherry, a lodging-house keeper, existing precariously upon a daily round of petty meannesses, was prepared for contest with a possible new boarder, who fortunately looked an unexperienced young gentleman.

'Someone has recommended me to you,' began Mrs Pennycherry. 'May I ask, who?'

But the stranger waved the question aside as immaterial.

'You might not remember—him,' he smiled. 'He thought that I should do well to pass the few months I am given—that I have to be in London, here. You can take me in?'

Mrs Pennycherry thought that she would be able to take the stranger in.

'A room to sleep in,' explained the stranger, '—any room will do—with food and drink sufficient for a man, is all that I require.'

'For breakfast,' began Mrs Pennycherry, 'I always give—'

'What is right and proper. I am convinced,' interrupted the stranger. 'Pray do not trouble to go into detail, Mrs Pennycherry. With whatever it is I shall be content.'

Mrs Pennycherry, puzzled, shot a quick glance at the stranger, but his face, though the gentle eyes were smiling, was frank and serious.

'At all events you will see the room,' suggested Mrs Pennycherry, 'before we discuss terms.'

'Certainly,' agreed the stranger. 'I am a little tired and shall be glad to rest there.'

Mrs Pennycherry led the way upward; on the landing of the third floor, paused a moment undecided, then opened the door of the back bedroom.

'It is very comfortable,' commented the stranger.

'For this room,' stated Mrs Pennycherry; 'together with full board, consisting of—'

'Of everything needful. It goes without saying,' again interrupted the stranger with his quiet grave smile.

'I have generally asked,' continued Mrs Pennycherry, 'four pounds a week. To you—' Mrs Pennycherry's voice, unknown to her, took to itself the note of aggressive generosity, 'seeing you have been recommended here, say three pound ten.'

'Dear lady,' said the stranger, 'that is kind of you. As you have divined, I am not a rich man. If it be not imposing upon you I accept your reduction with gratitude.'

Again Mrs Pennycherry, familiar with the satirical method, shot a suspicious glance upon the stranger, but not a line was there, upon that smooth fair face, to which a sneer could for a moment have clung. Clearly he was as simple as he looked.

'Gas, of course, extra.'

'Of course,' agreed the stranger.

'Coals—'

'We shall not quarrel,' for a third time the stranger interrupted. 'You have been very considerate to me as it is. I feel, Mrs Pennycherry, I can leave myself entirely in your hands.'

The stranger appeared anxious to be alone. Mrs Pennycherry, having put a match to the stranger's fire, turned to depart. And at this point it was that Mrs Pennycherry, the holder hitherto of an unbroken record for sanity, behaved in a manner she herself, five minutes earlier in her career, would have deemed impossible—that no living soul who had ever known her would have believed, even had Mrs Pennycherry gone down upon her knees and sworn it to them.

'Did I say three pound ten?' demanded Mrs Pennycherry of the stranger, her hand upon the door. She spoke crossly. She was feeling cross, with the stranger, with herself—particularly with herself.

'You were kind enough to reduce it to that amount,' replied the stranger, 'but if upon reflection you find yourself unable—'

'I was making a mistake,' said Mrs Pennycherry, should have been two pound ten.'

'I cannot—I will not accept such sacrifice,' exclaimed the stranger. 'The three pound ten I can well afford.'

'Two pound ten are my terms,' snapped Mrs Pennycherry. 'If you are bent on paying more, you can go elsewhere. You'll find plenty to oblige you.'

Her vehemence must have impressed the stranger. 'We will not contend further,' he smiled. 'I was merely afraid that in the goodness of your heart—'

'Oh, it isn't as good as all that,' growled Mrs Pennycherry.

'I am not so sure,' returned the stranger. 'I am somewhat suspicious of you. But wilful woman must, I suppose, have her way.'

The stranger held out his hand, and to Mrs Pennycherry, at that moment, it seemed the most natural thing in the world to take it as if it had been the hand of an old friend and to end the interview with a pleasant laugh—though laughing was an exercise not often indulged in by Mrs Pennycherry.

Mary Jane was standing by the window, her hands folded in front of her, when Mrs Pennycherry re-entered the kitchen. By standing close to the window one caught a glimpse of the trees in Bloomsbury Square and through their bare branches of the sky beyond.

'There's nothing much to do for the next half hour, till Cook comes back. I'll see to the door if you'd like a run out?' suggested Mrs Pennycherry.

'It would be nice,' agreed the girl so soon as she had recovered power of speech. 'It's just the time of day I like.'

'Don't be longer than the half hour,' added Mrs Pennycherry.

Forty-eight Bloomsbury Square, assembled after dinner in the drawing room, discussed the stranger with that freedom and frankness characteristic of Forty-eight Bloomsbury Square towards the absent.

'Not what I call a smart young man,' was the opinion of Augustus Longcord, who was something in the city.

'Thpeaking for mythelf,' commented his partner Isidore, 'hav'n'th any uthe for the thmart young man. Too many of him, ath it ith.'

'Must be pretty smart if he's one too many for you,' laughed his partner. There was this to be said for the repartee of Forty-eight Bloomsbury Square: it was simple of construction and easy of comprehension.

'Well it made me feel good just looking at him,' declared Miss Kite, the highly coloured. 'It was his clothes, I suppose—made me think of Noah and the ark—all that sort of thing.'

'It would be clothes that would make you think—if anything,' drawled the languid Miss Devine. She was a tall, handsome girl, engaged at the moment in futile efforts to recline with elegance and comfort combined upon a horsehair sofa. Miss Kite, by reason of having secured the only easy chair, was unpopular that evening; so that Miss Devine's remark received from the rest of the company more approbation than perhaps it merited.

'Is that intended to be clever, dear, or only rude?' Miss Kite requested to be informed.

'Both,' claimed Miss Devine.

'Myself, I must confess,' shouted the tall young lady's father, commonly called the Colonel, 'I found him a fool.'

'I noticed you seemed to be getting on very well together,' purred his wife, a plump smiling little lady.

'Possibly we were,' retorted the Colonel. 'Fate has accustomed me to the society of fools.'

'Isn't it a pity to start quarrelling immediately after dinner, you two,' suggested their thoughtful daughter from the sofa, 'you'll have nothing left to amuse you for the rest of the evening.'

'He didn't strike me as a conversationalist,' said the lady who was cousin to a baronet, 'but he did pass the vegetables before he helped himself. A little thing like that shows breeding.'

'Or that he didn't know you and thought maybe you'd leave him half a spoonful,' laughed Augustus the wit.

'What I can't make out about him—' shouted the Colonel.

The stranger entered the room.

The Colonel, securing the evening paper, retired into a corner. The highly coloured Kite, reaching down from the mantelpiece a paper fan, held it coyly before her face; Miss Devine sat upright on the horsehair sofa, and rearranged her skirts.

'Know anything?' demanded Augustus of the stranger, breaking the somewhat remarkable silence.

The stranger evidently did not understand. It was necessary for Augustus, the witty, to advance further into that odd silence.

'What's going to pull off the Lincoln Handicap? Tell me and I'll go out straight and put my shirt upon it.'

'I think you would act unwisely,' smiled the stranger. 'I am not an authority upon the subject.'

'Not! Why they told me you were Captain Spy of the *Sporting Life*—in disguise.'

It would have been difficult for a joke to fall more flat. Nobody laughed, though why Mr Augustus Longcord could not understand, and maybe none of his audience could have told him, for at Forty-eight Bloomsbury Square Mr Augustus Longcord passed as a humorist. The stranger himself appeared unaware that he was being made fun of.

'You have been misinformed,' assured him the stranger.

'I beg your pardon,' said Mr Augustus Longcord.

'It is nothing,' replied the stranger in his sweet low voice, and passed on.

'Well, what about this theatre?' demanded Mr Longcord of his friend and partner. 'Do you want to go or don't you?' Mr Longcord was feeling irritable.

'Goth the ticketh—may ath well,' thought Isidore.

'Damn stupid piece, I'm told.'

'Motht of them thupid, more or leth. Pity, to wathte the ticketh,' argued Isidore, and the pair went out.

'Are you staying long in London?' asked Miss Kite, raising her practised eyes towards the stranger.

'Not long,' answered the stranger. 'At least, I do not know. It depends.'

An unusual quiet had invaded the drawing room of Forty-eight Bloomsbury Square, generally noisy with strident voices about this hour. The Colonel remained engrossed in his paper. Mrs Devine sat with her plump white hands folded on her lap, whether asleep or not it was impossible to say. The lady who was cousin to a baronet had shifted her chair beneath the gasalier, her eyes bent on her everlasting crochet work. The languid Miss Devine had crossed to the piano, where she sat fingering softly the tuneless keys, her back to the cold barely furnished room.

'Sit down,' commanded saucily Miss Kite, indicating with her fan the vacant seat beside her. 'Tell me about yourself. You interest me.' Miss Kite adopted a pretty authoritative air towards all youthful-looking members of the opposite sex. It harmonized with the peach complexion and the golden hair, and fitted her about as well.

'I am glad of that,' answered the stranger, taking the chair suggested. 'I so wish to interest you.'

'You're a very bold boy,' Miss Kite lowered her fan, for the purpose of glancing archly over the edge of it, and for the first time encountered the eyes of the stranger looking into hers. And then it was that Miss Kite experienced precisely the same curious sensation that an hour or so ago had troubled Mrs Pennycherry when the stranger had first bowed to her. It seemed to Miss Kite that she was no longer the Miss Kite that, had she risen and looked into it, the flyblown mirror over the marble mantelpiece would, she knew, have presented to her view; but quite another Miss Kite—a cheerful, bright-eyed lady verging on middle age, yet still good-looking in spite of her faded complexion and somewhat thin brown locks. Miss Kite felt a pang of jealousy shoot through her; this middle-aged Miss Kite seemed, on the whole, a more attractive lady. There was a wholesomeness, a broadmindedness about her that instinctively drew one towards her. Not hampered, as Miss Kite herself was, by the necessity of appearing to be somewhere between eighteen and twenty-two, this other Miss Kite could talk sensibly, even brilliantly: one felt it. A thoroughly 'nice' woman this other Miss Kite; the real Miss Kite, though envious, was bound to admit it. Miss Kite wished to goodness she had never seen the woman. The glimpse of her had rendered Miss Kite dissatisfied with herself.

'I am not a boy,' exclaimed the stranger, 'and I had no intention of being bold.'

'I know,' replied Miss Kite. 'It was a silly remark. Whatever induced me to make it, I can't think. Getting foolish in my old age, I suppose.'

The stranger laughed. 'Surely you are not old.'

'I'm thirty-nine,' snapped out Miss Kite. 'You don't call it young?'

'I think it is a beautiful age,' insisted the stranger, 'young enough not to have lost the joy of youth, old enough to have learnt sympathy.'

'Oh I daresay,' returned Miss Kite, 'any age you'd think beautiful. I'm going to bed.' Miss Kite rose. The paper fan had somehow got itself broken. She threw the fragments into the fire.

'It is early yet,' pleaded the stranger, 'I was looking forward to a talk with you.'

'Well, you'll be able to look forward to it,' retorted Miss Kite. 'Good night.'

The truth was, Miss Kite was impatient to have a look at herself in the glass, in her own room with the door shut. The vision of that other Miss Kite—the clean-looking lady of the pale face and the brown hair had been so vivid, Miss Kite wondered whether temporary forgetfulness might not have fallen upon her while dressing for dinner that evening.

The stranger left to his own devices strolled towards the loo table, seeking something to read.

'You seem to have frightened away Miss Kite,' remarked the lady who was cousin to a baronet.

'It seems so,' admitted the stranger.

'My cousin, Sir William Bosster,' observed the crocheting lady, 'who married old Lord Egham's niece—you never met the Eghams?'

'Hitherto,' replied the stranger, 'I have not had that pleasure.'

'A charming family. Cannot understand—my cousin Sir William, I mean, cannot understand my remaining here. "My dear Emily"—he says the same thing every time he sees me—"My dear Emily, how can you exist among the sort of people one meets within a boarding house." But they amuse me.'

A sense of humour, agreed the stranger, was always of advantage.

'Our family on my mother's side,' continued Sir William's cousin in her placid monotone, 'was connected with the Tatton-Joneses, who when King George the Fourth—' Sir William's cousin, needing another reel of cotton, glanced up, and met the stranger's gaze.

'I'm sure I don't know why I'm telling you all this,' said Sir William's cousin in an irritable tone. 'It can't possibly interest you.'

'Everything connected with you interests me,' gravely the stranger assured her.

'It is very kind of you to say so,' sighed Sir William's cousin, but without conviction. 'I am afraid sometimes I bore people.'

The polite stranger refrained from contradiction.

'You see,' continued the poor lady, 'I really am of good family.'

'Dear lady,' said the stranger, 'your gentle face, your gentle voice, your gentle bearing, all proclaim it.'

She looked without flinching into the stranger's eyes, and gradually a smile banished the reigning dulness of her features.

'How foolish of me.' She spoke rather to herself than to the stranger. 'Why, of course, people—people whose opinion is worth troubling about—judge of you by what you are, not by what you go about saying you are.'

The stranger remained silent.

'I am the widow of a provincial doctor, with an income of just two hundred and thirty pounds per annum,' she argued. 'The sensible thing for me to do is to make the best of it, and to worry myself about these high and mighty relations of mine as little as they have ever worried themselves about me.'

The stranger appeared unable to think of anything worth saying.

'I have other connections,' remembered Sir William's cousin, 'those of my poor husband, to whom instead of being the "poor relation" I could be the fairy godmama. They are my people—or would be,' added Sir William's cousin tartly, 'if I wasn't a vulgar snob.'

She flushed the instant she had said the words and, rising, commenced preparations for a hurried departure.

'Now it seems I am driving you away,' sighed the stranger.

'Having been called a "vulgar snob,"' retorted the lady with some heat, 'I think it about time I went.'

'The words were your own,' the stranger reminded her.

'Whatever I may have thought,' remarked the indignant dame, 'no lady—least of all in the presence of a total stranger—would have called herself—'

The poor dame paused, bewildered. 'There is something very curious the matter with me this evening, that I cannot understand,' she explained. 'I seem quite unable to avoid insulting myself.'

Still surrounded by bewilderment, she wished the stranger good night, hoping that when next they met she would be more herself. The stranger, hoping so also, opened the door and closed it again behind her.

'Tell me,' laughed Miss Devine, who by sheer force of talent was contriving to wring harmony from the reluctant piano, 'how did you manage to do it? I should like to know.'

'How did I do what?' inquired the stranger.

'Contrive to get rid so quickly of those two old frumps?'

'How well you play!' observed the stranger. 'I knew you had genius for music the moment I saw you.'

'How could you tell?'

'It is written so clearly in your face.'

The girl laughed well pleased. 'You seem to have lost no time in studying my face.'

'It is a beautiful and interesting face,' observed the stranger.

She swung round sharply on the stool and their eyes met.

'You can read faces?'

'Yes.'

'Tell me, what else do you read in mine?'

'Frankness, courage—'

'Ah yes, all the virtues. Perhaps. We will take them for granted.' It was odd how serious the girl had suddenly become. 'Tell me the reverse side.'

'I see no reverse side,' replied the stranger. 'I see but a fair girl, bursting into noble womanhood.'

'And nothing else? You read no trace of greed, of vanity, of sordidness, of—' An angry laugh escaped her lips. 'And you are a reader of faces!'

'A reader of faces.' The stranger smiled. 'Do you know what is written upon yours at this very moment? A love of truth that is almost fierce, scorn of lies, scorn of hypocrisy, the desire for all things pure, contempt of all things that are contemptible—especially of such things as are contemptible in woman. Tell me, do I not read aright?'

I wonder, thought the girl, is that why those two others both hurried from the room? Does everyone feel ashamed of the littleness that is in them when looked at by those clear, believing eyes of yours?

The idea occurred to her: 'Papa seemed to have a good deal to say to you during dinner. Tell me, what were you talking about?'

'The military-looking gentleman upon my left? We talked about your mother principally.'

'I am sorry,' returned the girl, wishful now she had not asked the question. 'I was hoping he might have chosen another topic for the first evening!'

'He did try one or two,' admitted the stranger, 'but I have been about the world so little, I was glad when he talked to me about himself. I feel we shall be friends. He spoke so nicely, too, about Mrs Devine.'

'Indeed,' commented the girl.

'He told me he had been married for twenty years and had never regretted it but once!'

Her black eyes flashed upon him, but meeting his, the suspicion died from them. She turned aside to hide her smile.

'So he regretted it—once.'

'Only once,' explained the stranger, 'a passing irritable mood. It was so frank of him to admit it. He told me—I think he has taken a liking to me. Indeed he hinted as much. He said he did not often get an opportunity of talking to a man like myself—he told me that he and your mother, when they travel together, are always mistaken for a honeymoon couple. Some of the experiences he related to me were really quite amusing.' The stranger laughed at recollection of them—'that even here in this place, they are generally referred to as "Darby and Joan."'

'Yes, said the girl, 'that is true. Mr Longcord gave them that name, the second evening after our arrival. It was considered clever—but rather obvious I thought myself.'

'Nothing—so it seems to me,' said the stranger, 'is more beautiful than the love that has weathered the storms of life. The sweet, tender blossom that flowers in the heart of the young—in hearts such as yours—that, too, is beautiful. The love of the young for the young, that is the beginning of life. But the love of the old for the old, that is the beginning of—of things longer.'

'You seem to find all things beautiful,' the girl grumbled.

'But are not all things beautiful?' demanded the stranger. The Colonel had finished his paper. 'You two are engaged in a very absorbing conversation,' observed the Colonel
approaching them.

'We were discussing Darbies and Joans,' explained his daughter. 'How beautiful is the love that has weathered the storms of life!'

'Ah!' smiled the Colonel, 'that is hardly fair. My friend has been repeating to cynical youth the confessions of an amorous husband's affection for his middle-aged and somewhat—'The Colonel in playful mood laid his hand upon the stranger's shoulder, an action that necessitated his looking straight into the stranger's eyes. The Colonel drew himself up stiffly and turned scarlet.

Somebody was calling the Colonel a cad. Not only that, but was explaining quite clearly, so that the Colonel could see it for himself, why he was a cad.

'That you and your wife lead a cat and dog existence is a disgrace to both of you. At least you might have the decency to try and hide it from the world—not make a jest of your shame to every passing stranger. You are a cad, sir, a cad!'

Who was daring to say these things? Not the stranger, his lips had not moved. Besides, it was not his voice. Indeed it sounded much more like the voice of the Colonel himself. The Colonel looked from the stranger to his daughter, from his daughter back to the stranger. Clearly they had not heard the voice—a mere hallucination. The Colonel breathed again.

Yet the impression remaining was not to be shaken off. Undoubtedly it was bad taste to have joked to the stranger upon such a subject. No gentleman would have done so.

But then no gentleman would have permitted such a jest to be possible. No gentleman would be for ever wrangling with his wife—certainly never in public. However irritating the woman, a gentleman would have exercised self control.

Mrs Devine had risen, was coming slowly across the room. Fear laid hold of the Colonel. She was going to address some aggravating remark to him—he could see it in her eye—which would irritate him into savage retort. Even this prize idiot of a stranger would understand why boarding-house wits had dubbed them 'Darby and Joan', would grasp the fact that the gallant Colonel had thought it amusing, in conversation with a table acquaintance, to hold his own wife up to ridicule.

'My dear,' cried the Colonel, hurrying to speak first, 'does not this room strike you as cold? Let me fetch you a shawl.'

It was useless: the Colonel felt it. It had been too long the custom of both of them to preface with politeness their deadliest insults to each other. She came on, thinking of a suitable reply: suitable from her point of view, that is. In another moment the truth would be out. A wild, fantastic possibility flashed through the Colonel's brain: if to him, why not to her?

'Letitia,' cried the Colonel, and the tone of his voice surprised her into silence, 'I want you to look closely at our friend. Does he not remind you of someone?'

Mrs Devine, so urged, looked at the stranger long and hard. 'Yes,' she murmured, turning to her husband, 'he does, who is it?'

'I cannot fix it,' replied the Colonel. 'I thought that maybe you would remember.'

'It will come to me,' mused Mrs Devine. 'It is someone—years ago, when I was a girl—in Devonshire. Thank you, if it isn't troubling you, Harry. I left it in the dining room.'

It was, as Mr Augustus Longcord explained to his partner Isidore, the colossal foolishness of the stranger that was the cause of all the trouble.

'Give me a man, who can take care of himself—or thinks he can,' declared Augustus Longcord, 'and I am prepared to give a good account of myself. But when a helpless baby refuses even to look at what you call your figures, tells you that your mere word is sufficient for him, and hands you over his cheque book to fill up for yourself—well, it isn't playing the game.'

'Auguthtuth,' was the curt command of his partner, 'you're a fool.'

'All right, my boy, you try,' suggested Augustus. 'Jutht what I mean to do,' asserted his partner.

'Well,' demanded Augustus one evening later, meeting Isidore ascending the stairs after a long talk with the stranger in the dining room with the door shut.

'Oh don't arth me,' retorted Isidore, 'thilly ath, thath what he ith.'

'What did he say?'

'What did he thay! Talked about the Jewth: what a grand rathe they were—how people mithjudged them: all that thort of rot. Thaid thome of the motht honorable men he had ever met had been Jewth. Thought I wath one of 'em!'

'Well, did you get anything out of him?'

'Get anything out of him! Of courthe not. Couldn't very well thell the whole rathe, ath it were, for a couple of hundred poundth, after that. Didn't theem worth it.'

There were many things Forty-eight Bloomsbury Square came gradually to the conclusion were not worth the doing:—snatching at the gravy; pouncing out of one's turn upon the vegetables and helping oneself to more than one's fair share; manoeuvring for the easy chair; sitting on the evening paper while pretending not to have seen it—all such-like tiresome bits of business. For the little one made out of it, really it was not worth the bother. Grumbling everlastingly at one's food; grumbling everlastingly at most things; abusing Pennycherry behind her back; abusing, for a change, one's fellow-boarders; squabbling with one's fellow-boarders about nothing in particular; sneering at one's fellow-boarders; making senseless jokes about one's fellow-boarders; talking big about oneself, nobody believing one—all such-like vulgarities. Other boarding houses might indulge in them: Forty-eight Bloomsbury Square had its dignity to consider.

The truth is, Forty-eight Bloomsbury Square was coming to a very good opinion of itself: for the which not Bloomsbury Square so much as the stranger must be blamed. The stranger had arrived at Forty-eight Bloomsbury Square with the preconceived idea—where obtained from, Heaven knows—that its seemingly commonplace, mean-minded, coarse-fibred occupants were in reality ladies and gentlemen of the first water; and time and observation had apparently only strengthened this absurd idea. The natural result was, Forty-eight Bloomsbury Square was coming round to the stranger's opinion of itself.

Mrs Pennycherry the stranger would persist in regarding as a lady born and bred, compelled by circumstances over which she had no control to fill an arduous but honourable position in middle-class society—a sort of foster mother, to whom were due the thanks and gratitude of her promiscuous family; and this view of herself Mrs Pennycherry now clung to with obstinate conviction. There were disadvantages attaching, but these Mrs Pennycherry appeared prepared to suffer cheerfully. A lady born and bred cannot charge other ladies and gentlemen for coals and candles they have never burnt; a foster mother cannot palm off upon her children New Zealand mutton for Southdown. A mere lodging-house keeper can play these tricks, and pocket the profits. But a lady feels she cannot: Mrs Pennycherry felt she no longer could.

To the stranger, Miss Kite was a witty and delightful conversationalist of most attractive personality. Miss Kite had one failing: it was lack of vanity. She was unaware of her own delicate and refined beauty. If Miss Kite could only see herself with his, the stranger's, eyes, the modesty that rendered her distrustful of her natural charms would fall from her. The stranger was so sure of it Miss Kite determined to put it to the test. One evening, an hour before dinner, there entered the drawing room, when the stranger only was there and before the gas was lighted, a pleasant, good-looking lady, somewhat pale, with neatly arranged brown hair, who demanded of the stranger if he knew her. All her body was trembling, and her voice seemed inclined to run away from her and become a sob. But when the stranger, looking straight into her eyes, told her that from the likeness he thought she must be Miss Kite's younger sister, but much prettier, it became a laugh instead: and that evening the golden-haired Miss Kite disappeared never to show her highly coloured face again; and what perhaps, more than all else, might have impressed some former habitué of Forty-eight Bloomsbury Square with awe, was that no one in the house made even a passing inquiry concerning her.

Sir William's cousin the stranger thought an acquisition to any boarding-house. A lady of high-class family! There was nothing outward or visible perhaps to tell you that she was of high-class family. She herself, naturally, would not mention the fact, yet somehow you felt it. Unconsciously she set a high-class tone, diffused an atmosphere of gentle manners. Not that the stranger had said this in so many words; Sir William's cousin gathered that he thought it, and felt herself in agreement with him.

For Mr Longcord and his partner, as representatives of the best type of business men, the stranger had a great respect. With what unfortunate results to themselves has been noted. The curious thing is that the firm appeared content with the price they had paid for the stranger's good opinion—had even, it was rumoured, acquired a taste for honest men's respect, that in the long run was likely to cost them dear. But we all have our pet extravagance.

The Colonel and Mrs Devine both suffered a good deal at first from the necessity imposed upon them of learning, somewhat late in life, new tricks. In the privacy of their own apartment they condoled with one another.

'Tomfool nonsense,' grumbled the Colonel, 'you and I starting billing and cooing at our age!'

'What I object to,' said Mrs Devine, 'is the feeling that somehow I am being made to do it.'

'The idea that a man and his wife cannot have their little joke together for fear of what some impertinent jackanapes may think of them! It's damn ridiculous,' the Colonel exploded.

'Even when he isn't there,' said Mrs Devine, 'I seem to see him looking at me with those vexing eyes of his. Really the man quite haunts me.'

'I have met him somewhere,' mused the Colonel, 'I'll swear I've met him somewhere. I wish to goodness he would go.'

A hundred things a day the Colonel wanted to say to Mrs Devine, a hundred things a day Mrs Devine would have liked to observe to the Colonel. But by the time the opportunity occurred—when nobody else was by to hear—all interest in saying them was gone.

'Women will be women,' was the sentiment with which the Colonel consoled himself. 'A man must bear with them—must never forget that he is a gentleman.'

'Oh well, I suppose they're all alike,' laughed Mrs Devine to herself, having arrived at that stage of despair when one seeks refuge in cheerfulness. 'What's the use of putting oneself out—it does no good, and only upsets one.'

There is a certain satisfaction in feeling you are bearing with heroic resignation the irritating follies of others. Colonel and Mrs Devine came to enjoy the luxury of much self-approbation.

But the person seriously annoyed by the stranger's bigoted belief in the innate goodness of everyone he came across was the languid, handsome Miss Devine. The stranger would have it that Miss Devine was a noble-souled, high-minded young woman, something midway between a Flora Macdonald and a Joan of Arc. Miss Devine, on the contrary, knew herself to be a sleek, luxury-loving animal, quite willing to sell herself to the bidder who could offer her the finest clothes, the richest foods, the most sumptuous surroundings. Such a bidder was to hand in the person of a retired bookmaker, a somewhat greasy old gentleman, but exceedingly rich and undoubtedly fond.

Miss Devine, having made up her mind that the thing had got to be done, was anxious that it should be done quickly. And here it was that the stranger's ridiculous opinion of her not only irritated but inconvenienced her. Under the very eyes of a person—however foolish—convinced you are possessed of all the highest attributes of your sex, it is difficult to behave as though actuated by only the basest motives. A dozen times had Miss Devine determined to end the matter by formal acceptance of her elderly admirer's large and flabby hand, and a dozen times—the vision intervening of the stranger's grave, believing eyes—had Miss Devine refused decided answer. The stranger would one day depart. Indeed, he had told her himself, he was but a passing traveller. When he was gone it would be easier. So she thought at the time.

One afternoon, the stranger entered the room where she was standing by the window, looking out upon the bare branches of the trees in Bloomsbury Square. She remembered afterwards, it was just such another foggy afternoon as the afternoon of the stranger's arrival three months before. No one else was in the room. The stranger closed the door, and came towards her with that curious, quick leaping step of his. His long coat was tightly buttoned, and in his hands he carried his old felt hat, and the massive knotted stick that was almost a staff.

'I have come to say goodbye,' explained the stranger. 'I am going.'

'I shall not see you again?' asked the girl.

'I cannot say,' replied the stranger. 'But you will think of me?'

'Yes,' she answered with a smile. 'I can promise that.'

'And I shall always remember you,' promised the stranger, 'and I wish you every joy—the joy of love, the joy of a happy marriage.'

The girl winced. 'Love and marriage are not always the same thing,' she said.

'Not always,' agreed the stranger, 'but in your case they will be one.'

She looked at him.

'Do you think I have not noticed?' smiled the stranger, 'a gallant handsome lad, and clever. You love him and he loves you. I could not have gone away without knowing it was well with you.'

Her gaze wandered towards the fading light.

'Ah yes, I love him,' she answered petulantly. 'Your eyes can see clearly enough, when they want to. But one does not live on love, in our world. I will tell you the man I am going to marry if you care to know.' She would not meet his eyes. She kept her gaze still fixed upon the dingy trees, the mist beyond, and spoke rapidly and vehemently: 'The man who can give me all my soul's desire—money and the things that money can buy. You think me a woman, I'm only a pig. He is moist, and breathes like a porpoise; with cunning in place of a brain, and the rest of him mere stomach. But he is good enough for me.

She hoped this would shock the stranger and that now, perhaps, he would go. It irritated her to hear him only laugh.

'No,' he said, 'you will not marry him.'

'Who will stop me?' she cried angrily.

'Your better self.'

His voice had a strange ring of authority, compelling her to turn and look upon his face. Yes, it was true, the fancy that from the very first had haunted her. She had met him, talked to him—in silent country roads, in crowded city streets, where was it? And always in talking with him her spirit had been lifted up: she had been—what he had always thought her.

'There are those,' continued the stranger, and for the first time she saw that he was of a noble presence, that his gentle, childlike eyes could also command, 'whose better self lies slain by their own hand and troubles them no more. But yours, my child, you have let grow too strong, it will ever be your master. You must obey. Flee from it and it will follow you; you cannot escape it. Insult it and it will chastise you with burning shame, with stinging self-reproach from day to day.' The sternness faded from the beautiful face, the tenderness crept back. He laid his hand upon the young girl's shoulder.

'You will marry your lover,' he smiled. 'With him you will walk the way of sunlight and of shadow.'

And the girl, looking up into the strong, calm face, knew that it would be so, that the power of resisting her better self had passed away from her for ever.

'Now,' said the stranger, 'come to the door with me. Leave-takings are but wasted sadness. Let me pass out quietly. Close the door softly behind me.'

She thought that perhaps he would turn his face again, but she saw no more of him than the odd roundness of his back under the tightly buttoned coat, before he faded into the gathering fog.

Then softly she closed the door.

Diary of a Pilgrimage

I am lying in bed, or, to speak more truthfully, I am sitting up on a green satin, lace-covered pillow, writing these notes. A green satin, lace-covered bed is on the floor beside me. It is about eleven o'clock in the morning. B. is sitting up in his bed a few feet off, smoking a pipe. We have just finished a light repast of—what do you think? you will never guess—coffee and rolls. We intend to put the week straight by stopping in bed all day, at all events until the evening. Two English ladies occupy the bedroom next to ours. They seem to have made up their minds to also stay upstairs all day. We can hear them walking about their room, muttering. They have been doing this for the last three-quarters of an hour. They seem troubled about something.

It is very pleasant here. An overflow performance is being given in the theatre today for the benefit of those people who could not gain admittance yesterday, and, through the open windows, we can hear the rhythmic chant of the chorus. Mellowed by the distance, the wailing cadence of the plaintive songs, mingled with the shrill Haydnistic strains of the orchestra, falls with a mournful sweetness on our ears.

We ourselves saw the play yesterday, and we are now discussing it. I am explaining to B. the difficulty I experience in writing an account of it for my diary. I tell him that I do not know what to say about it.

He smokes for a while in silence, and then, taking the pipe from his lips, he says: 'Does it matter very much what you say about it?'

I find much relief in that thought. It at once lifts from my shoulders the oppressive feeling of responsibility that was weighing me down. After all, what does it matter what I say? What does it matter what any of us says about anything? Nobody takes much notice of it, luckily for everybody.

This reflection must be of great comfort to editors and critics. A conscientious man who really felt that his words would carry weight and influence with them would be almost afraid to speak at all. It is the man who knows that it will not make an ounce of difference to anyone what he says that can grow eloquent and vehement and positive. It will not make any difference to anybody or anything what I say about the Oberammergau Passion Play. So I shall just say what I want to.

But what do I want to say? What can I say that has not been said, and said much better, already? (An author must always pretend to think that every other author writes better than he himself does. He does not really think so, you know, but it looks well to talk as though he did.) What can I say that the reader does not know, or that, not knowing, he cares to know? It is easy enough to talk about nothing like I have been doing in this diary hitherto. It is when one is confronted with the task of writing about *something*, that one wishes one were a respectable well-to-do-sweep—a sweep with a comfortable business of his own, and a pony—instead of an author.

B. says: 'Well, why not begin by describing Oberammergau.'

I say it has been described so often.

He says: 'So has the Oxford and Cambridge Boat Race and the Derby Day, but people go on describing them all the same, and apparently find other people to read their descriptions. Say that the little village, clustered round its mosque-domed church, nestles in the centre of a valley, surrounded by great fir-robed hills, which stand, with the cross-crowned Kofel for their chief, like stern, strong sentinels guarding its old-world peace from the din and clamour of the outer world. Describe how the square, whitewashed houses are sheltered beneath great overhanging gables, and are encircled by carved wooden balconies and verandahs, where, in the cool of the evening, peasant wood-carver and peasant farmer sit to smoke the long Bavarian pipe, and chat about the cattle and the Passion Play and village politics; and how, in gaudy colours above the porch, are painted glowing figures of saints and virgins and such-like good folk, which the rains have sadly mutilated, so that a legless angel on one side of the road looks dejectedly across at a headless Madonna on the other, while at an exposed corner some unfortunate saint, more cruelly dealt with by the weather than he ever was even by the heathen, has been deprived of everything that he could call his own, with the exception of half a head and a pair of extra-sized feet.

'Explain how all the houses are numbered according to the date they were built, so that number sixteen comes next to number forty-seven, and there is no number one because it has been pulled down. Tell how unsophisticated visitors, informed that their lodgings are at number fifty-three, go wandering for days and days round fifty-two, under the not unreasonable impression that their house must be next door, though, as a matter of fact, it is half a mile off at the other end of the village, and are discovered one sunny morning, sitting on the doorstep of number eighteen, singing pathetic snatches of nursery rhymes, and trying to plat their toes into doormats, and are taken up and carried away screaming, to end their lives in the madhouse at Munich.

'Talk about the weather. People who have stayed here for any length of time tell me that it rains at Oberammergau three days out of every four, the reason that it does not rain on the fourth day being that every fourth day is set apart for a deluge. They tell me, also, that while it will be pouring with rain just in the village the sun will be shining brightly all round about, and that the villagers, when the water begins to come in through their roofs, snatch up their children and hurry off to the nearest field, where they sit and wait until the storm is over.'

'Do you believe them—the persons that you say tell you these tales?' I ask.

'Personally I do not,' he replies. 'I think people exaggerate to me because I look young and innocent, but no doubt there is a ground-work of truth in their statements. I have myself left Oberammergau under a steady drenching rain, and found a cloudless sky the other side of the Kofel.

'Then,' he continues, 'you can comment upon the hardihood of the Bavarian peasant. How he or she walks about bare-headed and bare-footed through the fiercest showers, and seems to find the rain only pleasantly cooling. How, during the performance of the Passion Play, they act and sing and stand about upon the uncovered stage without taking the slightest notice of the downpour of water that is soaking their robes and running from their streaming hair, to make great pools upon the boards; and how the audience, in the cheaper, unroofed portion of the theatre, sit with equal stoicism, watching them, no one ever dreaming even of putting up an umbrella—or, if he does dream of doing so, experiencing a very rude awakening from the sticks of those behind.'

B. stops to relight his pipe at this point, and I hear the two ladies in the next room fidgeting about and muttering worse than ever. It seems to me they are listening at the door (our room and theirs are connected by a door); I do wish that they would either get into bed again or else go downstairs. They worry me.

'And what shall I say after I have said all that?' I ask B. when at last he has started his pipe again.

'Oh! Well, after that,' he replies, 'you can give the history of the Passion Play; how it came to be played.'

'Oh, but so many people have done that already,' I say again.

'So much the better for you,' is his reply. 'Having previously heard precisely the same story from half a dozen other sources, the public will be tempted to believe you when you repeat the account. Tell them that during the Thirty Years' War a terrible plague (as if half a dozen different armies, marching up and down their country, fighting each other about the Lord only knows what, and living on them while doing it, was not plague enough) swept over Bavaria, devastating each town and hamlet. Of all the highland villages, Oberammergau by means of a strictly enforced quarantine alone kept, for a while, the black foe at bay. No soul was allowed to leave the village; no living thing to enter it.

'But one dark night Caspar Schuchler, an inhabitant of Oberammergau, who had been away working in the plague-stricken neighbouring village of Eschenlohe, creeping low on his belly, passed the drowsy sentinels, and gained his home, and saw what for many a day he had been hungering for—a sight of his wife and bairns. It was a selfish act to do, and he and his fellow-villagers paid dearly for it. Three days after he had entered his house he and all his family lay dead, and the plague was raging through the valley, and nothing seemed able to stay its course.

'When human means fail, we feel it is only fair to give Heaven a chance. The good people who dwelt by the side of the Ammer vowed that, if the plague left them, they would, every ten years, perform a Passion Play. The celestial powers seem to have at once closed with this offer. The plague disappeared as if by magic, and every recurring tenth year since, the Oberammergauites have kept their promise and played their Passion Play. They act it to this day as a pious observance. Before each performance all the characters gather together on the stage around their pastor, and, kneeling, pray for a blessing upon the work then about to commence. The profits that are made, after paying the performers a wage that just compensates them for their loss of time—wood-carver Maier, who plays the Christ, only receives about fifty pounds for the whole of the thirty or so performances given during the season, to say nothing of the winter's rehearsals—is put aside, part for the temporal benefit of the community, and the rest for the benefit of the Church. From burgomaster down to shepherd lad, from the Mary and the Jesus down to the meanest super, all work for the love of their religion, not for money. Each one feels that he is helping forward the cause of Christianity.'

'And I could also speak,' I add, 'of grand old Daisenberger, the gentle, simple old priest, "the father of the valley," who now lies in silence among his children that he loved so well. It was he, you know, that shaped the rude burlesque of a coarser age into the impressive reverential drama that we saw yesterday. That is a portrait of him over the bed. What a plain, homely, good face it is! How pleasant, how helpful it is to come across a good face now and then! I do not mean a sainted face, suggestive of stained glass and marble tombs, but a rugged human face that has had the grit, and rain, and sunshine of life rubbed into it, and that has gained its expression, not by looking up with longing at the stars, but by looking down with eyes full of laughter and love at the human things around it.'

'Yes,' assented B. 'You can put in that if you like. There is no harm in it. And then you can go on to speak of the play itself, and give your impressions concerning it. Never mind their being silly. They will be all the better for that. Silly remarks are generally more interesting than sensible ones.'

'But what is the use of saying anything about it at all?' I urge. 'The merest schoolboy must know all about the Oberammergau Passion Play by this time.'

'What has that to do with you?' answers B. 'You are not writing for cultured schoolboys. You are writing for mere simple men and women. They will be glad of a little information on the subject, and then when the schoolboy comes home for his holiday they will be able, so far as this topic, at all events, is concerned, to converse with him on his own level and not appear stupid.

'Come,' he says, kindly, trying to lead me on, 'what did you think about it?'

'Well,' I reply, after musing for a while, 'I think that a play of eighteen acts and some forty scenes, which commences at eight o'clock in the morning, and continues, with an interval of an hour and a half for dinner, until six o'clock in the evening, is too long. I think the piece wants cutting. About a third of it is impressive and moving, and what the earnest student of the drama at home is for ever demanding that a play should be—namely, elevating; but I consider that the other two thirds are tiresome.'

'Quite so,' answers B. 'But then we must remember that the performance is not intended as an entertainment, but as a religious service. To criticize any part of it as uninteresting is like saying that half the Bible might very well have been omitted, and that the whole story could have been told in a third of the space.

'And now, as to the right or wrong of the performance as a whole. Do you see any objection to the play from a religious point of view?'

'No,' I reply, 'I do not; nor do I understand how anybody else, and least of all a really believing Christian, can either. To argue as some do, that Christianity should be treated as a sacred mystery, is to argue against the whole scheme of Christianity. It was Christ himself that rent the veil of the Temple, and brought religion down into the streets and marketplaces of the world. Christ was a common man. He lived a common life, among common men and women. He died a common death. His own methods of teaching were what a Saturday reviewer, had he to deal with the case, would undoubtedly term vulgar. The roots of Christianity are planted deep down in the very soil of life, amid all that is commonplace, and mean, and petty, and everyday. Its strength lies in its simplicity, its homely humanness. It has spread itself through the world by speaking to the hearts, rather than to the heads of men. If it is still to live and grow, it must be helped along by such methods as these peasant players of Oberammergau employ, not by high-class essays and the learned discussions of the cultured.

'The crowded audience that sat beside us in the theatre yesterday saw Christ of Nazareth nearer than any book, however inspired, could bring him to them; clearer than any words, however eloquent, could show him. They saw the sorrow of his patient face. They heard his deep tones calling to them. They saw him in the hour of his so-called triumph, wending his way through the narrow streets of Jerusalem, the multitude that thronged round him waving their branches of green palms and shouting loud hosannas.

'What a poor scene of triumph!—a poor-clad, pale-faced man, mounted upon the back of a shuffling, unwilling little grey donkey, passing slowly through the byways of a city, busy upon other things. Beside him, a little band of worn, anxious men, clad in threadbare garments—fishermen, petty clerks, and the like; and, following, a noisy rabble, shouting, as crowds in all lands and in all times shout, and as dogs bark, they know not why—because others are shouting, or barking. And that scene marks the highest triumph won while he lived on earth by the village carpenter of Galilee, about whom the world has been fighting and thinking and talking so hard for the last eighteen hundred years.

'They saw him, angry and indignant, driving out the desecrators from the temple. They saw the rabble, who a few brief moments before had followed him, shouting "Hosanna," slinking away from him to shout with his foes.

'They saw the high priests in their robes of white, with the rabbis and doctors, all the great and learned in the land, sitting late into the night beneath the vaulted roof of the Sanhedrin's council hall, plotting his death.

'They saw him supping with his disciples in the house of Simon. They saw poor, loving Mary Magdalen wash his feet with costly ointment, that might have been sold for three hundred pence, and the money given to the poor—"and us." Judas was so thoughtful for the poor, so eager that other people should sell all they had, and give the money to the poor—"and us." Methinks that, even in this nineteenth century, one can still hear from many a tub and platform the voice of Judas, complaining of all waste, and pleading for the poor—"and us."

'They were present at the parting of Mary and Jesus by Bethany, and it will be many a day before the memory of that scene ceases to vibrate in their hearts. It is the scene that brings the humanness of the great tragedy most closely home to us. Jesus is going to face sorrow and death at Jerusalem. Mary's instinct tells her that this is so, and she pleads to him to stay.

'Poor Mary! To others he is the Christ, the Saviour of mankind, setting forth upon his mighty mission to redeem the world. To loving Mary Mother, he is her son: the baby she has suckled at her breast, the little one she has crooned to sleep upon her lap, whose little cheek has lain against her heart, whose little feet have made sweet music through the poor home at Bethany: he is her boy, her child; she would wrap her mother's arms around him, and hold him safe against all the world, against even heaven itself.

'Never, in any human drama, have I witnessed a more moving scene than this. Never has the voice of any actress (and I have seen some of the greatest, if any great ones are living) stirred my heart as did the voice of Rosa Lang, the burgomaster's daughter. It was not the voice of one woman, it was the voice of Motherdom, gathered together from all the world over.

'Oliver Wendell Holmes, in *The Autocrat of the Breakfast Table*, I think, confesses to having been bewitched at different times by two women's voices, and adds that both these voices belonged to German women. I am not surprised at either statement of the good doctor's. I am sure if a man did fall in love with a voice, he would find, on tracing it to its source, that it was the voice of some homely looking German woman. I have never heard such exquisite soul-drawing music in my life, as I have more than once heard float from the lips of some sweet-faced German Fraulein when she opened her mouth to speak. The voice has been so pure, so clear, so deep, so full of soft caressing tenderness, so strong to comfort, so gentle to soothe, it has seemed like one of those harmonies musicians tell us that they dream of, but can never chain to earth.

'As I sat in the theatre, listening to the wondrous tones of this mountain peasant woman, rising and falling like the murmur of a sea, filling the vast sky-covered building with their yearning notes, stirring like a great wind stirs Æolian strings, the thousands of trembling hearts around her, it seemed to me that I was indeed listening to the voice of the "mother of the world," of mother Nature herself.

'They saw him, as they had often seen him in pictures, sitting for the last time with his disciples at supper. But yesterday they saw him, not a mute, moveless figure, posed in conventional, meaningless attitude, but a living, loving man, sitting in fellowship with the dear friends that against all the world had believed in him, and had followed his poor fortunes, talking with them for the last sweet time, comforting them.

'They heard him bless the bread and wine that they themselves to this day take in remembrance of him.

'They saw his agony in the Garden of Gethsemane, the human shrinking from the cup of pain. They saw the false friend, Judas, betray him with a kiss. (Alas! Poor Judas! He loved Jesus, in a way, like the rest did. It was only his fear of poverty that made him betray his Master. He was so poor—he wanted the money so badly! We cry out in horror against Judas. Let us pray rather that we are never tempted to do a shameful action for a few pieces of silver. The fear of poverty ever did, and ever will, make scamps of men. We would like to be faithful, and noble, and just, only really times are so bad that we cannot afford it! As Becky Sharp says, it is so easy to be good and noble on five thousand a year, so very hard to be it on the mere five. If Judas had only been a well-to-do man, he might have been Saint Judas this day, instead of cursed Judas. He was not bad. He had only one failing—the failing that makes the difference between a saint and a villain, all the world over—he was a coward; he was afraid of being poor.)

'They saw him, pale and silent, dragged now before the priests of his own countrymen, and now before the Roman governor, while the voice of the people—the people who had cried "Hosanna" to him—shouted, "Crucify him! Crucify him!" They saw him bleeding from the crown of thorns. They saw him, still followed by the barking mob, sink beneath the burden of his cross. They saw the woman wipe the bloody sweat from off his face. They saw the last, long, silent look between the mother and the son, as, journeying upward to his death, he passed her in the narrow way through which he once had ridden in brief-lived triumph. They heard her low sob as she turned away, leaning on Mary Magdalen. They saw him nailed upon the cross between the thieves. They saw the blood start from his side. They heard his last cry to his God. They saw him rise victorious over death!

'Few believing Christians among the vast audience but must have passed out from that strange playhouse with their belief and love strengthened. The God of the Christian, for his sake, became a man, and lived and suffered and died as a man; and, as a man, living, suffering, dying among other men, he had that day seen him.

'The man of powerful imagination needs no aid from mimicry, however excellent, however reverent, to unroll before him in its simple grandeur the great tragedy on which the curtain fell at Calvary some eighteen and a half centuries ago.

'A cultivated mind needs no story of human suffering to win or hold it to a faith.

'But the imaginative and cultured are few and far between, and the peasants of Oberammergau can plead, as their Master himself once pleaded, that they seek not to help the learned but the lowly.

'The unbeliever, also, passes out into the village street full of food for thought. The rude sermon preached in this hillside temple has shown to him, clearer than he could have seen before, the secret wherein lies the strength of Christianity; the reason why, of all the faiths that Nature has taught to her children to help them in their need, to satisfy the hunger of their souls, this faith, born by the Sea of Galilee, has spread the farthest over the world, and struck its note the deepest into human life. Not by his doctrines, not even by his promises, has Christ laid hold upon the hearts of men but by the story of his life.'

The Street of the Blank Wall

I had turned off from the Edgware Road into a street leading west, the atmosphere of which had appealed to me. It was a place of quiet houses standing behind little gardens. They had the usual names printed on the stuccoed gateposts. The fading twilight was just sufficient to enable one to read them. There was a Laburnum Villa, and The Cedars, and a Cairngorm, rising to the height of three storeys, with a curious little turret that branched out at the top, and was crowned with a conical roof, so that it looked as if wearing a witch's hat. Especially when two small windows just below the eaves sprang suddenly into light, and gave one the feeling of a pair of wicked eyes suddenly flashed upon one.

The street curved to the right, ending in an open space through which passed a canal beneath a low-arched bridge. There were still the same quiet houses behind their small gardens, and I watched for a while the lamplighter picking out the shape of the canal, that widened just above the bridge into a lake with an island in the middle. After that I must have wandered in a circle, for later on I found myself back in the same spot, though I do not suppose I had passed a dozen people on my way; and then I set to work to find my way back to Paddington.

I thought I had taken the road by which I had come, but the half light must have deceived me. Not that it mattered. They had a lurking mystery about them, these silent streets with their suggestion of hushed move-ment behind drawn curtains, of whispered voices behind the flimsy walls. Occasionally there would escape the sound of laughter, suddenly stifled as it seemed, and once the sudden cry of a child.

It was in a short street of semidetached villas facing a high blank wall that, as I passed, I saw a blind move halfway up, revealing a woman's face.

A gas lamp, the only one the street possessed, was nearly opposite. I thought at first it was the face of a girl, and then, as I looked again, it might have been the face of an old woman. One could not distinguish the colouring. In any case, the cold, blue gaslight would have made it seem pallid.

The remarkable feature was the eyes. It might have been, of course, that they alone caught the light and held it, rendering them uncannily large and brilliant. Or it might have been that the rest of the face was small and delicate, out of all proportion to them. She may have seen me, for the blind was drawn down again, and I passed on.

There was no particular reason why, but the incident lingered with me. The sudden raising of the blind, as of the curtain of some small theatre, the barely furnished room coming dimly into view, and the woman standing there, close to the footlights, as to my fancy it seemed. And then the sudden ringing down of the curtain before the play had begun. I turned at the corner of the street. The blind had been drawn up again, and I saw again the slight, girlish figure silhouetted against the side panes of the bow window.

At the same moment a man knocked up against me. It was not his fault. I had stopped abruptly, not giving him time to avoid me. We both apologized, blaming the darkness. It may have been my fancy, but I had the feeling that, instead of going on his way, he had turned and was following me. I waited till the next corner, and then swung round on my heel. But there was no sign of him, and after a while I found myself back in the Edgware road.

Once or twice, in idle mood, I sought the street again, but without success; and the thing would, I expect, have faded from my memory, but that one evening, on my way home from Paddington, I came across the woman in the Harrow Road. There was no mistaking her. She almost touched me as she came out of a fishmonger's shop, and unconsciously, at the beginning, I found myself following her. This time I noticed the turnings, and five minutes' walking brought us to the street. Half a dozen times I must have been within a hundred yards of it. I lingered at the corner. She had not noticed me, and just as she reached the house a man came out of the shadows beyond the lamppost and joined her.

I was due at a bachelor gathering that evening, and after dinner, the affair being fresh in my mind, I talked about it. I am not sure, but I think it was in connection with a discussion on Maeterlinck. It was that sudden lifting of the blind that had caught hold of me. As if, blundering into an empty theatre, I had caught a glimpse of some drama being played in secret. We passed to other topics, and when I was leaving a fellow-guest asked me which way I was going. I told him, and, it being a fine night, he proposed that we should walk together. And in the quiet of Harley Street he confessed that his desire had not been entirely the pleasure of my company.

'It is rather curious,' he said, 'but today there suddenly came to my remembrance a case that for nearly eleven years I have never given a thought to. And now, on top of it, comes your description of that woman's face. I am wondering if it can be the same.'

'It was the eyes,' I said, 'that struck me as so remarkable.'

'It was the eyes that I chiefly remember her by,' he replied. 'Would you know the street again?'

We walked a little while in silence.

'It may seem, perhaps, odd to you,' I answered, 'but it would trouble me, the idea of any harm coming to her through me. What was the case?'

'You can feel quite safe on that point,' he assured me. 'I was her counsel—that is, if it is the same woman. How was she dressed?'

I could not see the reason for his question. He could hardly expect her to be wearing the clothes of eleven years ago.

'I don't think I noticed,' I answered. 'Some sort of a blouse, I suppose.' And then I recollected. 'Ah, yes, there was something uncommon,' I added. 'An unusually broad band of velvet, it looked like, round her neck.'

'I thought so,' he said. 'Yes. It must be the same.'

We had reached Marylebone Road, where our ways parted.

'I will look you up tomorrow afternoon, if I may,' he said. 'We might take a stroll round together.'

He called on me about half past five, and we reached the street just as the one solitary gas-lamp had been lighted. I pointed out the house to him, and he crossed over and looked at the number.

'Quite right,' he said, on returning. 'I made inquiries this morning. She was released six weeks ago on ticket of leave.'

He took my arm.

'Not much use hanging about,' he said. 'The blind won't go up tonight. Rather a clever idea, selecting a house just opposite a lamppost.'

He had an engagement that evening; but later on he told me the story—that is, so far as he then knew it.

It was in the early days of the garden suburb movement. One of the first sites chosen was off the Finchley Road. The place was in the building, and one of the streets—Laleham Gardens—had only some half a dozen houses in it, all unoccupied save one. It was a lonely, loose end of the suburb, terminating suddenly in open fields. From the unfinished end of the road the ground sloped down somewhat steeply to a pond, and beyond that began a small wood. The one house occupied had been bought by a young married couple named Hepworth.

The husband was a good-looking, pleasant young fellow. Being clean-shaven, his exact age was difficult to judge. The wife, it was quite evident, was little more than a girl. About the man there was a suggestion of weakness. At least, that was the impression left on the mind of the house agent. Today he would decide, and tomorrow he changed his mind. Jetson, the agent, had almost given up hope of bringing off a deal. In the end it was Mrs Hepworth who, taking the matter into her own hands, fixed upon the house in Laleham Gardens. Young Hepworth found fault with it on the ground of its isolation. He himself was often away for days at a time, travelling on business, and was afraid she would be nervous. He had been very persistent on this point; but in whispered conversations she had persuaded him out of his objection. It was one of those pretty, fussy little houses; and it seemed to have taken her fancy. Added to which, according to her argument, it was just within their means, which none of the others were. Young Hepworth may have given the usual references, but if so they were never taken up. The house was sold on the company's usual terms. The deposit was paid by a cheque, which was duly cleared, and the house itself was security for the rest. The company's solicitor, with Hepworth's consent, acted for both parties.

It was early in June when the Hepworths moved in. They furnished only one bedroom; and kept no servant, a charwoman coming in every morning and going away about six in the evening. Jetson was their nearest neighbour. His wife and daughters called on them, and confess to have taken a liking to them both. Indeed, between one of the Jetson girls, the youngest, and Mrs Hepworth there seems to have sprung up a close friendship. Young Hepworth, the husband, was always charming, and evidently took great pains to make himself agreeable. But with regard to him they had the feeling that he was never altogether at his ease. They described him—though that, of course, was after the event—as having left upon them the impression of a haunted man.

There was one occasion in particular. It was about ten o'clock. The Jetsons had been spending the evening with the Hepworths, and were just on the point of leaving, when there came a sudden, clear knock at the door. It turned out to be Jetson's foreman, who had to leave by an early train in the morning, and had found that he needed some further instructions. But the terror in Hepworth's face was unmistakable. He had turned a look towards his wife that was almost of despair; and it had seemed to the Jetsons—or, talking it over afterwards, they may have suggested the idea to each other—that there came a flash of contempt into her eyes, though it yielded the next instant to an expression of pity. She had risen, and already moved some steps towards the door, when young Hepworth had stopped her, and gone out himself. But the curious thing was that, according to the foreman's account, Hepworth never opened the front door, but came upon him stealthily from behind. He must have slipped out by the back and crept round the house.

The incident had puzzled the Jetsons, especially that involuntary flash of contempt that had come into Mrs Hepworth's eyes. She had always appeared to adore her husband, and of the two, if possible, to be the one most in love with the other. They had no friends or acquaintances except the Jetsons. No one else among their neighbours had taken the trouble to call on them, and no stranger to the suburb had, so far as was known, ever been seen in Laleham Gardens.

Until one evening a little before Christmas.

Jetson was on his way home from his office in the Finchley Road. There had been a mist hanging about all day, and with nightfall it had settled down into a whitish fog. Soon after leaving the Finchley Road, Jetson noticed in front of him a man wearing a long, yellow mackintosh, and some sort of soft felt hat. He gave Jetson the idea of being a sailor; it may have been merely the stiff, serviceable mackintosh. At the corner of Laleham Gardens the man turned, and glanced up at the name upon the lamppost, so that Jetson had a full view of him. Evidently it was the street for which he was looking. Jetson, somewhat curious, the Hepworths' house being still the only one occupied, paused at the corner, and watched. The Hepworths' house was, of course, the only one in the road that showed any light. The man, when he came to the gate, struck a match for the purpose of reading the number. Satisfied it was the house he wanted, he pushed open the gate and went up the path.

But, instead of using the bell or knocker, Jetson was surprised to hear him give three raps on the door with his stick. There was no answer, and Jetson, whose interest was now thoroughly aroused, crossed to the other corner, from where he could command a better view. Twice the man repeated his three raps on the door, each time a little louder, and the third time the door was opened. Jetson could not tell by whom, for whoever it was kept behind it.

He could just see one wall of the passage, with a pair of old naval cutlasses crossed above the picture of a three-masted schooner that he knew hung there. The door was opened just sufficient, and the man slipped in, and the door was closed behind him. Jetson had turned to continue his way, when the fancy seized him to give one glance back. The house was in complete darkness, though a moment before Jetson was positive there had been a light in the ground-floor window.

It all sounded very important afterwards, but at the time there was nothing to suggest to Jetson anything very much out of the common. Because for six months no friend or relation had called to see them, that was no reason why one never should. In the fog, a stranger may have thought it simpler to knock at the door with his stick than to fumble in search of a bell. The Hepworths lived chiefly in the room at the back. The light in the drawing room may have been switched off for economy's sake. Jetson recounted the incident on reaching home, not as anything remarkable, but just as one mentions an item of gossip. The only one who appears to have attached any meaning to the affair was Jetson's youngest daughter, then a girl of eighteen. She asked one or two questions about the man, and, during the evening, slipped out by herself and ran round to the Hepworths. She found the house empty. At all events, she could obtain no answer, and the place, back and front, seemed to her to be uncannily silent.

Jetson called the next morning, something of his daughter's uneasiness having communicated itself to him. Mrs Hepworth herself opened the door to him. In his evidence at the trial, Jetson admitted that her appearance had startled him. She seems to have anticipated his questions by at once explaining that she had had news of an unpleasant nature, and had been worrying over it all night. Her husband had been called away suddenly to America, where it would be necessary for her to join him as soon as possible. She would come round to Jetson's office later in the day to make arrangements about getting rid of the house and furniture.

The story seemed reasonably to account for the stranger's visit, and Jetson, expressing his sympathy and promising all help in his power, continued his way to the office. She called in the afternoon and handed him over the keys, retaining one for herself. She wished the furniture to be sold by auction, and he was to accept almost any offer for the house. She would try and see him again before sailing; if not, she would write him with her address. She was perfectly cool and collected. She had called on his wife and daughters in the afternoon, and had wished them goodbye.

Outside Jetson's office she hailed a cab, and returned in it to Laleham Gardens to collect her boxes. The next time Jetson saw her she was in the dock, charged with being an accomplice in the murder of her husband.

The body had been discovered in a pond some hundred yards from the unfinished end of Laleham Gardens. A house was in course of erection on a neighbouring plot, and a workman, in dipping up a pail of water, had dropped in his watch. He and his mate, worrying round with a rake, had drawn up pieces of torn clothing, and this, of course, had led to the pond being properly dragged. Otherwise the discovery might never have been made.

The body, heavily weighted with a number of flat irons fastened to it by a chain and padlock, had sunk deep into the soft mud, and might have remained there till it rotted. A valuable gold repeater, that Jetson remembered young Hepworth having told him had been a presentation to his father, was in its usual pocket, and a cameo ring that Hepworth had always worn on his third finger was likewise fished up from the mud. Evidently the murder belonged to the category of crimes passionel. The theory of the prosecution was that it had been committed by a man who, before her marriage, had been Mrs Hepworth's lover.

The evidence, contrasted with the almost spiritually beautiful face of the woman in the dock, came as a surprise to everyone in court. Originally connected with an English circus troupe touring in Holland, she appears, about seventeen, to have been engaged as a 'song and dance artiste' at a particularly shady *café chantant* in Rotterdam, frequented chiefly by sailors. From there a man, an English sailor known as Charlie Martin, took her away, and for some months she had lived with him at a small *estaminet* the other side of the river. Later, they left Rotterdam and came to London, where they took lodgings in Poplar, near to the docks.

It was from this address in Poplar that, some ten months before the murder, she had married young Hepworth. What had become of Martin was not known. The natural assumption was that, his money being exhausted, he had returned to his calling, though his name, for some reason, could not be found in any ship's list.

That he was one and the same with the man that Jetson had watched till the door of the Hepworths' house had closed upon him there could be no doubt. Jetson described him as a thickset, handsome-looking man, with a reddish beard and moustache. Earlier in the day he had been seen at Hampstead, where he had dined at a small coffee shop in the High Street. The girl who had waited on him had also been struck by the bold, piercing eyes and the curly red beard. It had been an off time, between two and three, when he had dined there, and the girl admitted that she had found him a 'pleasant-spoken gentleman,' and 'inclined to be merry.' He had told her that he had arrived in England only three days ago, and that he hoped that evening to see his sweetheart. He had accompanied the words with a laugh, and the girl thought—though, of course, this may have been after-suggestion—that an ugly look followed the laugh.

One imagines that it was this man's return that had been the fear constantly haunting young Hepworth. The three raps on the door, it was urged by the prosecution, was a pre-arranged or pre-understood signal, and the door had been opened by the woman. Whether the husband was in the house, or whether they waited for him, could not be said. He had been killed by a bullet entering through the back of the neck; the man had evidently come prepared.

Ten days had elapsed between the murder and the finding of the body, and the man was never traced. A postman had met him coming from the neighbourhood of Laleham Gardens at about half past nine. In the fog, they had all but bumped into one another, and the man had immediately turned away his face.

About the soft felt hat there was nothing to excite attention, but the long, stiff, yellow mackintosh was quite unusual. The postman had caught only a momentary glimpse of the face, but was certain it was clean shaven. This made a sensation in court for the moment, but only until the calling of the next witness. The charwoman usually employed by the Hepworths had not been admitted to the house on the morning of Mrs Hepworth's departure. Mrs Hepworth had met her at the door and paid her a week's money in lieu of notice, explaining to her that she would not be wanted any more. Jetson, thinking he might possibly do better by letting the house furnished, had sent for this woman, and instructed her to give the place a thorough cleaning. Sweeping the carpet in the dining room with a dustpan and brush, she had discovered a number of short red hairs. The man, before leaving the house, had shaved himself.

That he had still retained the long, yellow mackintosh may have been with the idea of starting a false clue. Having served its purpose, it could be discarded. The beard would not have been so easy. What roundabout way he may have taken one cannot say, but it must have been some time during the night or early morning that he reached young Hepworth's office in Fenchurch Street. Mrs Hepworth had evidently provided him with the key.

There he seems to have hidden the hat and mackintosh and to have taken in exchange some clothes belonging to the murdered man. Hepworth's clerk, Ellenby, an elderly man—of the type that one generally describes as of gentlemanly appearance—was accustomed to his master being away unexpectedly on business, which was that of a ships' furnisher. He always kept an overcoat and a bag ready packed in the office. Missing them, Ellenby had assumed that his master had been called away by an early train. He would have been worried after a few days, but that he had received a telegram—as he then supposed from his master—explaining that young Hepworth had gone to Ireland and would be away for some days. It was nothing unusual for Hepworth to be absent, superintending the furnishing of a ship, for a fortnight at a time, and nothing had transpired in the office necessitating special instructions. The telegram had been handed in at Charing Cross, but the time chosen had been a busy period of the day, and no one had any recollection of the sender. Hepworth's clerk unhesitatingly identified the body as that of his employer, for whom it was evident that he had entertained a feeling of affection. About Mrs Hepworth he said as little as he could. While she was awaiting her trial it had been necessary for him to see her once or twice with reference to the business. Previous to this, he knew nothing about her.

The woman's own attitude throughout the trial had been quite unexplainable. Beyond agreeing to a formal plea of not guilty, she had made no attempt to defend herself. What little assistance her solicitors had obtained had been given them, not by the woman herself, but by Hepworth's clerk, more for the sake of his dead master than out of any sympathy towards the wife. She herself appeared utterly indifferent. Only once had she been betrayed into a momentary emotion. It was when her solicitors were urging her almost angrily to give them some particulars upon a point they thought might be helpful to her case.

'He's dead!' she had cried out almost with a note of exultation. 'Dead! Dead! What else matters?'

The next moment she had apologized for her outburst. 'Nothing can do any good,' she had said. 'Let the thing take its course.'

It was the astounding callousness of the woman that told against her both with the judge and the jury. That shaving in the dining room, the murdered man's body not yet cold! It must have been done with Hepworth's safety razor. She must have brought it down to him, found him a looking glass, brought him soap and water and a towel, afterwards removing all traces. Except those few red hairs that had clung, unnoticed, to the carpet. That nest of flat irons used to weight the body! It must have been she who had thought of them. The idea would never have occurred to a man. The chain and padlock with which to fasten them. She only could have known that such things were in the house. It must have been she who had planned the exchange of clothes in Hepworth's office, giving him the key. She it must have been who had thought of the pond, holding open the door while the man had staggered out under his ghastly burden; waited, keeping watch, listening to hear the splash.

Evidently it had been her intention to go off with the murderer—to live with him! That story about America. If all had gone well, it would have accounted for everything. After leaving Laleham Gardens she had taken lodgings in a small house in Kentish Town under the name of Howard, giving herself out to be a chorus singer, her husband being an actor on tour. To make the thing plausible, she had obtained employment in one of the pantomimes. Not for a moment had she lost her head. No one had ever called at her lodgings, and there had come no letters for her. Every hour of her day could be accounted for. Their plans must have been worked out over the corpse of her murdered husband. She was found guilty of being an accessory after the fact, and sentenced to fifteen years' penal servitude.

That brought the story up to eleven years ago. After the trial, interested in spite of himself, my friend had ferreted out some further particulars. Inquiries at Liverpool had procured him the information that Hepworth's father, a ship-owner in a small way, had been well known and highly respected. He was retired from business when he died, some three years previous to the date of the murder. His wife had survived him by only a few months. Besides Michael, the murdered son, there were two other children—an elder brother, who was thought to have gone abroad to one of the colonies, and a sister who had married a French naval officer. Either they had not heard of the case or had not wished to have their names dragged into it. Young Michael had started life as an architect, and was supposed to have been doing well, but after the death of his parents had disappeared from the neighbourhood, and, until the trial, none of his acquaintances up north ever knew what had become of him.

But a further item of knowledge that my friend's inquiries had elicited had somewhat puzzled him. Hepworth's clerk, Ellenby, had been the confidential clerk of Hepworth's father! He had entered the service of the firm as a boy; and when Hepworth senior retired, Ellenby—with the old gentleman's assistance—had started in business for himself as a ships' furnisher! Nothing of all this came out at the trial. Ellenby had not been cross-examined. There was no need for it. But it seemed odd, under all the circumstances, that he had not volunteered the information. It may, of course, have been for the sake of the brother and sister. Hepworth is a common enough name in the north. He may have hoped to keep the family out of connection with the case.

As regards the woman, my friend could learn nothing further beyond the fact that, in her contract with the music-hall agent in Rotterdam, she had described herself as the daughter of an English musician, and had stated that both her parents were dead. She may have engaged herself without knowing the character of the hall, and the man, Charlie Martin, with his handsome face and pleasing sailor ways, and at least an Englishman, may have seemed to her a welcome escape.

She may have been passionately fond of him, and young Hepworth—crazy about her, for she was beautiful enough to turn any man's head—may in Martin's absence have lied to her, told her he was dead—lord knows what!—to induce her to marry him. The murder may have seemed to her a sort of grim justice.

But even so, her cold-blooded callousness was surely abnormal! She had married him, lived with him for nearly a year. To the Jetsons she had given the impression of being a woman deeply in love with her husband. It could not have been mere acting kept up day after day.

'There was something else.' We were discussing the case in my friend's chambers. His brief of eleven years ago was open before him. He was pacing up and down with his hands in his pockets, thinking as he talked. 'Something that never came out. There was a curious feeling she gave me in that moment when sentence was pronounced upon her. It was as if, instead of being condemned, she had triumphed. Acting! If she had acted during the trial, pretended remorse, even pity, I could have got her off with five years. She seemed to be unable to disguise the absolute physical relief she felt at the thought that he was dead, that his hand would never again touch her. There must have been something that had suddenly been revealed to her, something that had turned her love to hate.

'There must be something fine about the man, too.' That was another suggestion that came to him as he stood staring out of the window across the river. 'She's paid and has got her receipt, but he is still wanted. He is risking his neck every evening he watches for the raising of that blind.'

His thought took another turn.

'Yet how could he have let her go through those ten years of living death while he walked the streets scot free? Some time during the trial— the evidence piling up against her day by day—why didn't he come forward, if only to stand beside her? Get himself hanged, if only out of mere decency?'

He sat down, took the brief up in his hand without looking at it.

'Or was that the reward that she claimed? That he should wait, keeping alive the one hope that would make the suffering possible to her? Yes,' he continued, musing, 'I can see a man who cared for a woman taking that as his punishment.'

Now that his interest in the case had been revived he seemed unable to keep it out of his mind. Since our joint visit I had once or twice passed through the street by myself, and on the last occasion had again seen the raising of the blind. It obsessed him—the desire to meet the man face to face. A handsome, bold, masterful man, he conceived him. But there must be something more for such a woman to have sold her soul—almost, one might say—for the sake of him.

There was just one chance of succeeding. Each time he had come from the direction of the Edgware Road. By keeping well out of sight at the other end of the street, and watching till he entered it, one might time oneself to come upon him just under the lamp. He would hardly be likely to turn and go back; that would be to give himself away. He would prob- ably content himself with pretending to be like ourselves, merely hurrying through, and in his turn watching till we had disappeared.

Fortune seemed inclined to favour us. About the usual time the blind was gently raised, and very soon afterwards there came round the corner the figure of a man. We entered the street ourselves a few seconds later, and it seemed likely that, as we had planned, we should come face to face with him under the gaslight. He walked towards us, stooping and with bent head. We expected him to pass the house by. To our surprise he stopped when he came to it, and pushed open the gate. In another moment we should have lost all chance of seeing anything more of him except his bent back. With a couple of strides my friend was behind him. He laid his hand on the man's shoulder and forced him to turn round. It was an old, wrinkled face with gentle, rather watery eyes.

We were both so taken aback that for a moment we could say nothing. My friend stammered out an apology about having mistaken the house, and rejoined me. At the corner we burst out laughing almost simultaneously. And then my friend suddenly stopped and stared at me.

'Hepworth's old clerk!' he said. 'Ellenby!'

It seemed to him monstrous. The man had been more than a clerk. The family had treated him as a friend. Hepworth's father had set him up in business. For the murdered lad he had had a sincere attachment; he had left that conviction on all of them. What was the meaning of it?

A directory was on the mantelpiece. It was the next afternoon. I had called upon him in his chambers. It was just an idea that came to me. I crossed over and opened it, and there was his name, 'Ellenby and Co., Ships' Furnishers', in a court off the Minories.

Was he helping her for the sake of his dead master—trying to get her away from the man. But why? The woman had stood by and watched the lad murdered. How could he bear even to look on her again?

Unless there had been that something that had not come out—something he had learnt later—that excused even that monstrous callousness of hers.

Yet what could there be? It had all been so planned, so cold-blooded. That shaving in the dining room! It was that seemed most to stick in his throat. She must have brought him down a looking glass; there was not one in the room. Why couldn't he have gone upstairs into the bathroom, where Hepworth always shaved himself, where he would have found everything to his hand?

He had been moving about the room, talking disjointedly as he paced, and suddenly he stopped and looked at me.

'Why in the dining room?' he demanded of me.

He was jingling some keys in his pocket. It was a habit of his when cross-examining, and I felt as if somehow I knew; and, without thinking—so it seemed to me—I answered him.

'Perhaps,' I said, 'it was easier to bring a razor down than to carry a dead man up.'

He leant with his arms across the table, his eyes glittering with excitement.

'Can't you see it?' he said. 'That little back parlour with its fussy ornaments. The three of them standing round the table, Hepworth's hands nervously clutching a chair. The reproaches, the taunts, the threats. Young Hepworth—he struck everyone as a weak man, a man physically afraid—white, stammering, not knowing which way to look. The woman's eyes turning from one to the other. That flash of contempt again—she could not help it—followed, worse still, by pity. If only he could have answered back, held his own! If only he had not been afraid! And then that fatal turning away with a sneering laugh one imagines, the bold, dominating eyes no longer there to cow him.

'That must have been the moment. The bullet, if you remember, entered through the back of the man's neck. Hepworth must always have been picturing to himself this meeting—tenants of garden suburbs do not carry loaded revolvers as a habit—dwelling upon it till he had worked himself up into a frenzy of hate and fear. Weak men always fly to extremes. If there was no other way, he would kill him.

'Can't you hear the silence? After the reverberations had died away! And then they are both down on their knees, patting him, feeling for his heart. The man must have gone down like a felled ox; there were no traces of blood on the carpet. The house is far from any neighbour; the shot in all probability has not been heard. If only they can get rid of the body! The pond—not a hundred yards away!'

He reached for the brief, still lying among his papers; hurriedly turned the scored pages.

'What easier? A house being built on the very next plot. Wheelbarrows to be had for the taking. A line of planks reaching down to the edge. Depth of water where the body was discovered four feet six inches. Nothing to do but just tip up the barrow.

'Think a minute. Must weigh him down, lest he rise to accuse us; weight him heavily, so that he will sink lower and lower into the soft mud, lie there till he rots.

'Think again. Think it out to the end. Suppose, in spite of all our precautions, he does rise? Suppose the chain slips? The workmen going to and fro for water—suppose they do discover him?

'He is lying on his back, remember. They would have turned him over to feel for his heart. Have closed his eyes, most probably, not liking their stare.

'It would be the woman who first thought of it. She has seen them both lying with closed eyes beside her. It may have always been in her mind, the likeness between them. With Hepworth's watch in his pocket, Hepworth's ring on his finger! If only it was not for the beard—that fierce, curling, red beard!

'They creep to the window and peer out. Fog still thick as soup. Not a soul, not a sound. Plenty of time.

'Then to get away, to hide till one is sure. Put on the mackintosh. A man in a yellow mackintosh may have been seen to enter; let him be seen to go away. In some dark corner or some empty railway carriage take it off and roll it up. Then make for the office. Wait there for Ellenby. True as steel, Ellenby; good business man. Be guided by Ellenby.'

He flung the brief from him with a laugh.

'Why, there's not a missing link!' he cried. 'And to think that not a fool among us ever thought of it!'

'Everything fitting into its place,' I suggested, 'except young Hepworth. Can you see him, from your description of him, sitting down and coolly elaborating plans for escape, the corpse of the murdered man stretched beside him on the hearthrug?'

'No,' he answered. 'But I can see her doing it, a woman who for week after week kept silence while we raged and stormed at her, a woman who for three hours sat like a statue while old Cutbush painted her to a crowded court as a modern Jezebel, who rose up from her seat when that sentence of fifteen years' penal servitude was pronounced upon her with a look of triumph in her eyes, and walked out of court as if she had been a girl going to meet her lover.

'I'll wager,' he added, 'it was she who did the shaving. Hepworth would have cut him, even with a safety razor.'

'It must have been the other one, Martin,' I said, 'that she loathed. That almost exultation at the thought that he was dead,' I reminded him.

'Yes,' he mused. 'She made no attempt to disguise it. Curious there having been that likeness between them.' He looked at his watch. 'Do you care to come with me?' he said.

'Where are you going?' I asked him.

'We may just catch him,' he answered. 'Ellenby and Co.'

The office was on the top floor of an old-fashioned house in a cul-de-sac off the Minories. Mr Ellenby was out, so the lanky office boy informed us, but would be sure to return before evening; and we sat and waited by the meagre fire till, as the dusk was falling, we heard his footsteps on the creaking stairs.

He halted a moment in the doorway, recognizing us apparently without surprise; and then, with a hope that we had not been kept waiting long, he led the way into an inner room.

'I do not suppose you remember me,' said my friend, as soon as the door was closed. 'I fancy that, until last night, you never saw me without my wig and gown. It makes a difference. I was Mrs Hepworth's senior counsel.'

It was unmistakable, the look of relief that came into the old, dim eyes. Evidently the incident of the previous evening had suggested to him an enemy.

'You were very good,' he murmured. 'Mrs Hepworth was overwrought at the time, but she was very grateful, I know, for all your efforts.'

I thought I detected a faint smile on my friend's lips.

'I must apologize for my rudeness to you of last night,' he continued. 'I expected, when I took the liberty of turning you round, that I was going to find myself face to face with a much younger man.'

'I took you to be a detective,' answered Ellenby, in his soft, gentle voice. 'You will forgive me, I'm sure. I am rather short-sighted. Of course, I can only conjecture, but if you will take my word, I can assure you that Mrs Hepworth has never seen or heard from the man Charlie Martin since the date of—he hesitated a moment—'of the murder.'

'It would have been difficult,' agreed my friend, 'seeing that Charlie Martin lies buried in Highgate Cemetery.'

Old as he was, he sprang from his chair, white and trembling.

'What have you come here for?' he demanded.

'I took more than a professional interest in the case,' answered my friend. 'Ten years ago I was younger than I am now. It may have been her youth—her extreme beauty. I think Mrs Hepworth, in allowing her husband to visit her—here where her address is known to the police, and watch at any moment may be set upon her—is placing him in a position of grave danger. If you care to lay before me any facts that will allow me to judge of the case, I am prepared to put my experience, and, if need be, my assistance, at her service.'

His self-possession had returned to him.

'If you will excuse me,' he said, 'I will tell the boy that he can go.'

We heard him, a moment later, turn the key in the outer door; and when he came back and had made up the fire, he told us the beginning of the story.

The name of the man buried in Highgate Cemetery was Hepworth, after all. Not Michael, but Alex, the elder brother.

From boyhood he had been violent, brutal, unscrupulous. Judging from Ellenby's story, it was difficult to accept him as a product of modern civilization. Rather he would seem to have been a throwback to some savage, buccaneering ancestor. To expect him to work, while he could live in vicious idleness at somebody else's expense, was found to be hopeless. His debts were paid for about the third or fourth time, and he was shipped off to the Colonies. Unfortunately, there were no means of keeping him there. So soon as the money provided him had been squandered, he returned, demanding more by menaces, and threats. Meeting with unexpected firmness, he seems to have regarded theft and forgery as the only alternatives left to him. To save him from punishment and the family name from disgrace, his parents' savings were sacrificed. It was grief and shame that, according to Ellenby, killed them both within a few months of one another.

Deprived by this blow of what he no doubt had come to consider his natural means of support, and his sister, fortunately for herself, being well out of his reach, he next fixed upon his brother Michael as his stay-by. Michael, weak, timid, and not perhaps without some remains of boyish affection for a strong, handsome, elder brother, foolishly yielded. The demands, of course, increased, until, in the end, it came almost as a relief when the man's vicious life led to his getting mixed up with a crime of a particularly odious nature. He was anxious now for his own sake to get away, and Michael, with little enough to spare for himself, provided him with the means, on the solemn understanding that he would never return.

But the worry and misery of it all had left young Michael a broken man. Unable to concentrate his mind any longer upon his profession, his craving was to get away from all his old associations—to make a fresh start in life. It was Ellenby who suggested London and the ship furnishing business, where Michael's small remaining capital would be of service. The name of Hepworth would be valuable in shipping circles, and Ellenby, arguing this consideration, but chiefly with the hope of giving young Michael more interest in the business, had insisted that the firm should be Hepworth and Co.

They had not been started a year before the man returned, as usual demanding more money. Michael, acting under Ellenby's guidance, refused in terms that convinced his brother that the game of bullying was up. He waited a while, and then wrote pathetically that he was ill and starving. If only for the sake of his young wife, would not Michael come and see them?

This was the first they had heard of his marriage. There was just a faint hope that it might have effected a change, and Michael, against Ellenby's advice, decided to go. In a miserable lodging house in the East End he found the young wife, but not his brother, who did not return till he was on the point of leaving. In the interval the girl seems to have confided her story to Michael.

She had been a singer, engaged at a music hall in Rotterdam. There Alex Hepworth, calling himself Charlie Martin, had met her and made love to her. When he chose, he could be agreeable enough, and no doubt her youth and beauty had given to his protestations, for the time being, a genuine ring of admiration and desire. It was to escape from her surroundings, more than anything else, that she had consented. She was little more than a child, and anything seemed preferable to the nightly horror to which her life exposed her.

He had never married her. At least, that was her belief at the time. During his first drunken bout he had flung it in her face that the form they had gone through was mere bunkum. Unfortunately for her, this was a lie. He had always been coolly calculating. It was probably with the idea of a safe investment that he had seen to it that the ceremony had been strictly legal.

Her life with him, so soon as the first novelty of her had worn off, had been unspeakable. The band that she wore round her neck was to hide where, in a fit of savagery because she had refused to earn money for him on the streets, he had tried to cut her throat. Now that she had got back to England she intended to leave him. If he followed and killed her she did not care.

It was for her sake that young Hepworth eventually offered to help his brother again, on the condition that he would go away—by himself. To this the other agreed. He seems to have given a short display of remorse. There must have been a grin on his face as he turned away. His cunning eyes had foreseen what was likely to happen. The idea of blackmail was no doubt in his mind from the beginning. With the charge of bigamy as a weapon in his hand, he might rely for the rest of his life upon a steady and increasing income.

Michael saw his brother off as a second-class passenger on a ship bound for the Cape. Of course, there was little chance of his keeping his word, but there was always the chance of his getting himself knocked on the head in some brawl. Anyhow, he would be out of the way for a season, and the girl, Lola, would be left. A month later he married her, and four months after that received a letter from his brother containing messages to Mrs Martin, 'from her loving husband, Charlie,' who hoped before long to have the pleasure of seeing her again.

Inquiries through the English consul in Rotterdam proved that the threat was no mere bluff. The marriage had been legal and binding.

What happened on the night of the murder was very much as my friend had reconstructed it. Ellenby, reaching the office at his usual time the next morning, had found Hepworth waiting for him. There he had remained in hiding until one morning, with dyed hair and a slight moustache, he had ventured forth.

Had the man's death been brought about by any other means, Ellenby would have counselled his coming forward and facing his trial, as he himself was anxious to do; but, viewed in conjunction with the relief the man's death must have been to both of them, that loaded revolver was too suggestive of premeditation. The isolation of the house, that conveniently near pond, would look as if thought of beforehand. Even if, pleading extreme provocation, Michael escaped the rope, a long term of penal servitude would be inevitable.

Nor was it certain that even then the woman would go free. The murdered man would still, by a strange freak, be her husband; the murderer—in the eye of the law—her lover.

Her passionate will had prevailed. Young Hepworth had sailed for America. There he had no difficulty in obtaining employment—of course, under another name—in an architect's office; and later had set up for himself. Since the night of the murder they had not seen each other till some three weeks ago.

I never saw the woman again. My friend, I believe, called on her. Hepworth had already returned to America, and my friend had succeeded in obtaining for her some sort of a police permit that practically left her free.

Sometimes of an evening I find myself passing through the street. And always I have the feeling of having blundered into an empty theatre—where the play is ended.

His Evening Out

The evidence of the park-keeper, David Bristow, of Gilder Street, Camden Town, is as follows:

I was on duty in St James's Park on Thursday evening, my sphere extending from the Mall to the northern shore of the ornamental water east of the suspension bridge. At five and twenty to seven I took up a position between the peninsula and the bridge to await my colleague. He ought to have relieved me at half past six, but did not arrive until a few minutes before seven, owing, so he explained, to the breaking down of his motor-bus—which may have been true or may not, as the saying is.

I had just come to a halt, when my attention was arrested by a lady. I am unable to explain why the presence of a lady in St James's Park should have seemed in any way worthy of notice except that, for certain reasons, she reminded me of my first wife. I observed that she hesitated between one of the public seats and two vacant chairs standing by themselves a little farther to the east. Eventually she selected one of the chairs, and, having cleaned it with an evening paper—the birds in this portion of the park being extremely prolific—sat down upon it. There was plenty of room upon the public seat close to it, except for some children who were playing touch; and in consequence of this I judged her to be a person of means.

I walked to a point from where I could command the southern approaches to the bridge, my colleague arriving sometimes by way of Birdcage Walk and sometimes by way of the Horse Guards Parade. Not seeing any signs of him in the direction of the bridge, I turned back. A little way past the chair where the lady was sitting I met Mr Parable. I know Mr Parable quite well by sight. He was wearing the usual grey suit and soft felt hat with which the pictures in the newspapers have made us all familiar. I judged that Mr Parable had come from the Houses of Parliament, and the next morning my suspicions were confirmed by reading that he had been present at a tea-party given on the terrace by Mr Will Crooks. Mr Parable conveyed to me the suggestion of a man absorbed in thought, and not quite aware of what he was doing; but in this, of course, I may have been mistaken. He paused for a moment to look over the railings at the pelican. Mr Parable said something to the pelican which I was not near enough to overhear; and then, still apparently in a state of abstraction, crossed the path and seated himself on the chair next to that occupied by the young lady.

From the tree against which I was standing I was able to watch the subsequent proceedings unobserved. The lady looked at Mr Parable and then turned away and smiled to herself. It was a peculiar smile, and, again in some way I am unable to explain, reminded me of my first wife. It was not till the pelican put down his other leg and walked away that Mr Parable, turning his gaze westward, became aware of the lady's presence.

From information that has subsequently come to my knowledge, I am prepared to believe that Mr Parable, from the beginning, really thought the lady was a friend of his. What the lady thought is a matter for conjecture; I can only speak to the facts. Mr Parable looked at the lady once or twice. Indeed, one might say with truth that he kept on doing it. The lady, it must be admitted, behaved for a while with extreme propriety; but after a time, as I felt must happen, their eyes met, and then it was I heard her say: 'Good evening, Mr Parable.'

She accompanied the words with the same peculiar smile to which I have already alluded. The exact words of Mr Parable's reply I cannot remember. But it was to the effect that he had thought from the first that he had known her but had not been quite sure.

It was at this point that, thinking I saw my colleague approaching, I went to meet him. I found I was mistaken, and slowly retraced my steps. I passed Mr Parable and the lady. They were talking together with what I should describe as animation. I went as far as the southern extremity of the suspension bridge, and must have waited there quite ten minutes before returning eastward. It was while I was passing behind them on the grass, partially screened by the rhododendrons, that I heard Mr Parable say to the lady: 'Why shouldn't we have it together?'

To which the lady replied: 'But what about Miss Clebb?'

I could not overhear what followed, owing to their sinking their voices. It seemed to be an argument. It ended with the young lady laughing and then rising. Mr Parable also rose, and they walked off together. As they passed me I heard the lady say: 'I wonder if there's any place in London where you're not likely to be recognized.'

Mr Parable, who gave me the idea of being in a state of growing excitement, replied quite loudly: 'Oh, let 'em!'

I was following behind them when the lady suddenly stopped.

'I know!' she said. 'The Popular Café.'

The park-keeper said he was convinced he would know the lady again, having taken particular notice of her. She had brown eyes and was wearing a black hat supplemented with poppies.

Arthur Horton, waiter at the Popular Café, states as follows:

I know Mr John Parable by sight. Have often heard him speak at public meetings. Am a bit of a Socialist myself. Remember his dining at the Popular Café on the evening of Thursday. Didn't recognize him immediately on his entrance for two reasons. One was his hat, and the other was his girl. I took it from him and hung it up. I mean, of course, the hat. It was a brand-new bowler, a trifle ikey about the brim. Have always associated him with a soft grey felt. But never with girls. Females, yes, to any extent. But this was the real article. You know what I mean—the sort of girl that you turn round to look after. It was she who selected the table in the corner behind the door. Been there before, I should say.

I should, in the ordinary course of business, have addressed Mr Parable by name, such being our instructions in the case of customers known to us. But, putting the hat and the girl together, I decided not to. Mr Parable was all for our three-and-six penny table d'hôte; he evidently not wanting to think. But the lady wouldn't hear of it.

'Remember Miss Clebb,' she reminded him.

Of course, at the time I did not know what was meant. She ordered thin soup, a grilled sole, and cutlets au gratin. It certainly couldn't have been the dinner. With regard to the champagne, he would have his own way. I picked him out a dry '94, that you might have weaned a baby on. I suppose it was the whole thing combined.

It was after the sole that I heard Mr Parable laugh. I could hardly credit my ears, but halfway through the cutlets he did it again.

There are two kinds of women. There is the woman who, the more she eats and drinks, the stodgier she gets, and the woman who lights up after it. I suggested a pêche Melba between them, and when I returned with it, Mr Parable was sitting with his elbows on the table gazing across at her with an expression that I can only describe as quite human. It was when I brought the coffee that he turned to me and asked: 'What's doing? Nothing stuffy,' he added. 'Is there an exhibition anywhere—something in the open air?'

'You are forgetting Miss Clebb,' the lady reminded him.

'For two pins,' said Mr Parable, 'I would get up at the meeting and tell Miss Clebb what I really think about her.'

I suggested the Earl's Court Exhibition, little thinking at the time what it was going to lead to; but the lady at first wouldn't hear of it, and the party at the next table calling for their bill (they had asked for it once or twice before, when I came to think of it), I had to go across to them.

When I got back the argument had just concluded, and the lady was holding up her finger.

'On condition that we leave at half past nine, and that you go straight to Caxton Hall,' she said.

'We'll see about it,' said Mr Parable, and offered me half a crown.

Tips being against the rules, I couldn't take it. Besides, one of the jumpers had his eye on me. I explained to him, jocosely, that I was doing it for a bet. He was surprised when I handed him his hat, but, the lady whispering to him, he remembered himself in time.

As they went out together I heard Mr Parable say to the lady: 'It's funny what a shocking memory I have for names.'

To which the lady replied: 'You'll think it funnier still tomorrow.' And then she laughed.

Mr Horton thought he would know the lady again. He puts down her age at about twenty-six, describing her—to use his own piquant expression—as 'a bit of all right.' She had brown eyes and a taking way with her.

Miss Ida Jenks, in charge of the Eastern Cigarette Kiosk at the Earl's Court Exhibition, gives the following particulars:

From where I generally stand I can easily command a view of the interior of the Victoria Hall; that is, of course, to say when the doors are open, as on a warm night is usually the case.

On the evening of Thursday, the twenty-seventh, it was fairly well occupied, but not to any great extent. One couple attracted my attention by reason of the gentleman's erratic steering. Had he been my partner I should have suggested a polka, the tango not being the sort of dance that can be picked up in an evening. What I mean to say is, that he struck me as being more willing than experienced. Some of the bumps she got would have made me cross; but we all have our fancies, and, so far as I could judge, they both appeared to be enjoying themselves. It was after the 'Hitchy Koo' that they came outside.

The seat to the left of the door is popular by reason of its being partly screened by bushes, but by leaning forward a little it is quite possible for me to see what goes on there. They were the first couple out, having had a bad collision near the bandstand, so easily secured it. The gentleman was laughing.

There was something about him from the first that made me think I knew him, and when he took off his hat to wipe his head it came to me all of a sudden, he being the exact image of his effigy at Madame Tussaud's, which, by a curious coincidence, I happened to have visited with a friend that very afternoon. The lady was what some people would call good-looking, and others mightn't.

I was watching them, naturally a little interested. Mr Parable, in helping the lady to adjust her cloak, drew her—it may have been by accident—towards him; and then it was that a florid gentleman with a short pipe in his mouth stepped forward and addressed the lady. He raised his hat and, remarking 'Good evening,' added that he hoped she was 'having a pleasant time.' His tone, I should explain, was sarcastic.

The young woman, whatever else may be said of her, struck me as behaving quite correctly. Replying to his salutation with a cold and distant bow, she rose, and, turning to Mr Parable, observed that she thought it was perhaps time for them to be going.

The gentleman, who had taken his pipe from his mouth, said—again in a sarcastic tone—that he thought so too, and offered the lady his arm.

'I don't think we need trouble you,' said Mr Parable, and stepped between them.

To describe what followed I, being a lady, am hampered for words. I remember seeing Mr Parable's hat go up into the air, and then the next moment the florid gentleman's head was lying on my counter smothered in cigarettes. I naturally screamed for the police, but the crowd was dead against me; and it was only after what I believe in technical language would be termed 'the fourth round' that they appeared upon the scene.

The last I saw of Mr Parable he was shaking a young constable who had lost his helmet, while three other policemen had hold of him from behind. The florid gentleman's hat I found on the floor of my kiosk and returned to him; but after a useless attempt to get it on his head, he disappeared with it in his hand. The lady was nowhere to be seen.

Miss Jenks thinks she would know her again. She was wearing a hat trimmed with black chiffon and a spray of poppies, and was slightly freckled.

Superintendent S. Wade, in answer to questions put to him by our representative, vouchsafed the following replies:

Yes. I was in charge at the Vine Street Police Station on the night of Thursday, the twenty-seventh.

No. I have no recollection of a charge of any description being preferred against any gentleman of the name of Parable.

Yes. A gentleman was brought in about ten o'clock charged with brawling at the Earl's Court Exhibition and assaulting a constable in the discharge of his duty.

The gentleman gave the name of Mr Archibald Quincey, Harcourt Buildings, Temple.

No. The gentleman made no application respecting bail, electing to pass the night in the cells. A certain amount of discretion is permitted to us, and we made him as comfortable as possible.

Yes. A lady.

No. About a gentleman who had got himself into trouble at the Earl's Court Exhibition. She mentioned no name.

I showed her the charge sheet. She thanked me and went away.

That I cannot say. I can only tell you that at nine-fifteen on Friday morning bail was tendered, and, after inquiries, accepted in the person of Julius Addison Tupp, of the Sunnybrook Steam Laundry, Twickenham.

That is no business of ours.

The accused who, I had seen to it, had had a cup of tea and a little toast at seven-thirty, left in company with Mr Tupp soon after ten.

Superintendent. Wade admitted he had known cases where accused parties, to avoid unpleasantness, had stated their names to be other than their own, but declined to discuss the matter further.

Superintendent Wade, while expressing his regret that he had no more time to bestow upon our representative, thought it highly probable that he would know the lady again if he saw her.

Without professing to be a judge of such matters, Superintendent Wade thinks she might be described as a highly intelligent young woman, and of exceptionally prepossessing appearance.

From Mr Julius Tupp, of the Sunnybrook Steam Laundry, Twickenham, upon whom our representative next called, we have been unable to obtain much assistance, Mr Tupp replying to all questions put to him by the one formula, 'Not talking.'

Fortunately, our representative, on his way out through the drying ground, was able to obtain a brief interview with Mrs Tupp.

Mrs Tupp remembers admitting a young lady to the house on the morning of Friday, the twenty-eighth, when she opened the door to take in the milk. The lady, Mrs Tupp remembers, spoke in a husky voice, the result, as the young lady explained with a pleasant laugh, of having passed the night wandering about Ham Common, she having been misdirected the previous evening by a fool of a railway porter, and not wishing to disturb the neighbourhood by waking people up at two o'clock in the morning, which, in Mrs Tupp's opinion, was sensible of her.

Mrs Tupp describes the young lady as of agreeable manners, but looking, naturally, a bit washed out. The lady asked for Mr Tupp, explaining that a friend of his was in trouble, which did not in the least surprise Mrs Tupp, she herself not holding with Socialists and such like. Mr Tupp, on being informed, dressed hastily and went downstairs, and he and the young lady left the house together. Mr Tupp, on being questioned as to the name of his friend, had called up that it was no one Mrs Tupp would know, a Mr Quince—it may have been Quincey.

Mrs Tupp is aware that Mr Parable is also a Socialist, and is acquainted with the saying about thieves hanging together. But has worked for Mr Parable for years and has always found him a most satisfactory client; and, Mr Tupp appearing at this point, our representative thanked Mrs Tupp for her information and took his departure.

Mr Horatius Condor Junior, who consented to partake of luncheon in company with our representative at the Holborn Restaurant, was at first disinclined to be of much assistance, but eventually supplied our representative with the following information:

My relation to Mr Archibald Quincey, Harcourt Buildings, Temple, is perhaps a little difficult to define.

How he himself regards me I am never quite sure. There will be days together when we will be quite friendly like, and at other times he will be that offhanded and peremptory you might think I was his blooming office boy.

On Friday morning, the twenty-eighth, I didn't get to Harcourt Buildings at the usual time, knowing that Mr Quincey would not be there himself, he having arranged to interview Mr Parable for the *Daily Chronicle* at ten o'clock. I allowed him half an hour, to be quite safe, and he came in at a quarter past eleven.

He took no notice of me. For about ten minutes—it may have been less—he walked up and down the room, cursing and swearing and kicking the furniture about. He landed an occasional walnut table in the middle of my shins, upon which I took.the opportunity of wishing him 'Good morning,' and he sort of woke up, as you might say.

'How did the interview go off?' I says. 'Got anything interesting?'

'Yes,' he said, 'quite interesting. Oh, yes, decidedly interesting.'

He was holding himself in, if you understand, speaking with horrible slowness and deliberation.

'D'you know where he was last night?' he asks me.

'Yes,' I says, 'Caxton Hall, wasn't it?—Meeting to demand the release of Miss Clebb.'

He leans across the table till his face was within a few inches of mine.

'Guess again,' he says.

I wasn't doing any guessing. He had hurt me with the walnut table, and I was feeling a bit short-tempered.

'Oh! don't make a game of it,' I says. 'It's too early in the morning.'

'At the Earl's Court Exhibition,' he says, 'dancing the tango with a lady that he picked up in St James's Park.'

'Well,' I says, 'why not? He don't often get much fun.' I thought it best to treat it lightly.

He takes no notice of my observation.

'A rival comes upon the scene,' he continues—'a fatheaded ass, according to my information—and they have a stand-up fight. He gets run in and spends the night in a Vine Street police cell.'

I suppose I was grinning without knowing it.

'Funny, ain't it?' he says.

'Well,' I says, 'it has its humorous side, hasn't it? What'll he get?'

'I am not worrying about what *he* is going to get,' he answers back. 'I am worrying about what *I* am going to get.'

I thought he had gone dotty.

'What's it got to do with you?' I says.

'If old Wotherspoon is in a good humour,' he continues, 'and the constable's head has gone down a bit between now and Wednesday, I may get off with forty shillings and a public reprimand.

'On the other hand,' he goes on—he was working himself into a sort of fit—'if the constable's head goes on swelling, and old Wotherspoon's liver gets worse, I've got to be prepared for a month without the option. That is, if I am fool enough—'

He had left both the doors open, which in the daytime we generally do, our chambers being at the top. Miss Dorton—that's Mr Parable's secretary—barges into the room. She didn't seem to notice me. She staggers to a chair and bursts into tears.

'He's gone,' she says, 'he's taken Cook with him and gone.'

'Gone!' says the guv'nor. 'Where's he gone?'

'To Fingest,' she says through her sobs—'to the cottage. Miss Bulstrode came in just after you had left,' she says. 'He wants to get away from everyone and have a few days' quiet. And then he is coming back, and he is going to do it himself.'

'Do what?' says the guv'nor, irritable like. 'Fourteen days,' she wails. 'It'll kill him.'

'But the case doesn't come on till Wednesday,' says the guv'nor. 'How do you know it's going to be fourteen days?'

'Miss Bulstrode,' she says, 'she's seen the magistrate. He says he always gives fourteen days in cases of unprovoked assault.'

'But it wasn't unprovoked,' says the guv'nor. 'The other man began it by knocking off his hat. It was self-defence.'

'She put that to him,' she says, 'and he agreed that that would alter his view of the case. But, you see,' she continues, 'we can't find the other man. He isn't likely to come forward of his own accord.'

'The girl must know,' says the guv'nor—'this girl he picks up in St James's Park and goes dancing with. The man must have been some friend of hers.'

'But we can't find her either,' she says. 'He doesn't even know her name—he can't remember it.'

'You will do it, won't you?' she says.

'Do what?' says the guv'nor again.

'The fourteen days,' she says.

'But I thought you said he was going to do it himself?' he says.

'But he mustn't,' she says. 'Miss Bulstrode is coming round to see you. Think of it! Think of the headlines in the papers,' she says. 'Think of the Fabian Society. Think of the Suffrage cause. We mustn't let him.'

'What about me?' says the guv'nor. 'Doesn't anybody care for me?'

'You don't matter,' she says. 'Besides,' she says, 'with your influence you'll be able to keep it out of the papers. If it comes out that it was Mr Parable, nothing on earth will be able to.'

The guv'nor was almost as much excited by this time as she was.

'I'll see the Fabian Society and the Women's Vote and the Home for Lost Cats at Battersea, and all the rest of the blessed bag of tricks—'

I'd been thinking to myself, and had just worked it out.

'What's he want to take his cook down with him for?' I says.

'To cook for him,' says the guv'nor. 'What d'you generally want a cook for?'

'Rats!' I says. 'Does he usually take his cook with him?'

'No,' answered Miss Dorton. 'Now I come to think of it, he has always hitherto put up with Mrs Meadows.'

'You will find the lady down at Fingest,' I says, 'sitting opposite him and enjoying a recherché dinner for two.'

The guv'nor slaps me on the back, and lifts Miss Dorton out of her chair.

'You get on back,' he says, 'and telephone to Miss Bulstrode. I'll be round at half past twelve.'

Miss Dorton went out in a dazed sort of condition, and the guv'nor gives me a sovereign, and tells me I can have the rest of the day to myself.

Mr Condor Junior considers that what happened subsequently goes to prove that he was right more than it proves that he was wrong.

Mr Condor Junior also promised to send us a photograph of himself for reproduction, but, unfortunately, up to the time of going to press it had not arrived.

From Mrs Meadows, widow of the late Corporal John Meadows, vc, Turberville, Bucks, the following further particulars were obtained by our local representative:

I have done for Mr Parable now for some years past, my cottage being only a mile off, which makes it easy for me to look after him.

Mr Parable likes the place to be always ready so that he can drop in when he chooses, he sometimes giving me warning and sometimes not. It was about the end of last month—on a Friday, if I remember rightly—that he suddenly turned up.

As a rule, he walks from Henley Station, but on this occasion he arrived in a fly, he having a young woman with him, and she having a bag—his cook, as he explained to me. As a rule, I do everything for Mr Parable, sleeping in the cottage when he is there; but to tell the truth, I was glad to see her. I never was much of a cook myself, as my poor dead husband has remarked on more than one occasion, and I don't pretend to be. Mr Parable added, apologetic like, that he had been suffering lately from indigestion.

'I am only too pleased to see her,' I says. 'There are the two beds in my room, and we shan't quarrel.' She was quite a sensible young woman, as I had judged from the first look at her, though suffering at the time from a cold. She hires a bicycle from Emma Tidd, who only uses it on a Sunday, and, taking a market basket, off she starts for Henley, Mr Parable saying he would go with her to show her the way.

They were gone a goodish time, which, seeing it's eight miles, didn't so much surprise me; and when they got back we all three had dinner together, Mr Parable arguing that it made for what he called 'labour saving.' Afterwards I cleared away, leaving them talking together; and later on they had a walk round the garden, it being a moonlight night, but a bit too cold for my fancy.

In the morning I had a chat with her before he was down. She seemed a bit worried.

'I hope people won't get talking,' she says. 'He would insist on my coming.'

'Well,' I says, 'surely a gent can bring his cook along with him to cook for him. And as for people talking, what I always say is, one may just as well give them something to talk about and save them the trouble of making it up.'

'If only I was a plain, middle-aged woman,' she says, 'it would be all right.'

'Perhaps you will be, all in good time,' I says, but, of course, I could see what she was driving at. A nice, clean, pleasant-faced young woman she was, and not of the ordinary class. 'Meanwhile,' I says, 'if you don't mind taking a bit of motherly advice, you might remember that your place is the kitchen, and his the parlour. He's a dear good man, I know, but human nature is human nature, and it's no good pretending it isn't.'

She and I had our breakfast together before he was up, so that when he came down he had to have his alone, but afterwards she comes into the kitchen and closes the door.

'He wants to show me the way to High Wycombe,' she says. 'He will have it there are better shops at Wycombe. What ought I to do?'

My experience is that advising folks to do what they don't want to do isn't the way to do it.

'What d'you think yourself?' I asked her.

'I feel like going with him,' she says, 'and making the most of every mile.'

And then she began to cry.

'What's the harm!' she says. 'I have heard him from a dozen platforms ridiculing class distinctions. Besides,' she says, 'my people have been farmers for generations. What was Miss Bulstrode's father but a grocer? He ran a hundred shops instead of one. What difference does that make?'

'When did it all begin?' I says. 'When did he first take notice of you like?'

'The day before yesterday,' she answers. 'He had never seen me before,' she says. 'I was just "Cook"—something in a cap and apron that he passed occasionally on the stairs. On Thursday he saw me in my best clothes, and fell in love with me. He doesn't know it himself, poor dear, not yet, but that's what he's done.'

Well, I couldn't contradict her, not after the way I had seen him looking at her across the table.

'What are your feelings towards him,' I says, 'to be quite honest? He's rather a good catch for a young person in your position.'

'That's my trouble,' she says. 'I can't help thinking of that. And then to be Mrs John Parable! That's enough to turn a woman's head.'

'He'd be a bit difficult to live with,' I says.

'Geniuses always are,' she says. It's easy enough if you just think of them as children. He'd be a bit fractious at times, that's all. Underneath, he's just the kindest, dearest—'

'Oh, you take your basket and go to High Wycombe,' I says. 'He might do worse.'

I wasn't expecting them back soon, and they didn't come back soon. In the afternoon a motor stops at the gate, and out of it steps Miss Bulstrode, Miss Dorton—that's the young lady that writes for him—and Mr Quincey. I told them I couldn't say when he'd be back, and they said it didn't matter, they just happening to be passing.

'Did anybody call on him yesterday?' asks Miss Bulstrode, careless like—
'A lady?'

'No,' I says, 'you are the first as yet.'

'He's brought his cook down with him, hasn't he?' says Mr Quincey.

'Yes,' I says, 'and a very good cook too,' which was the truth.

'I'd like just to speak a few words with her,' says Miss Bulstrode.

'Sorry, m'am,' I says, 'but she's out at present. She's gone to Wycombe.'

'To market,' I says. 'It's a little farther, but, of course, it stands to reason the shops there are better.'

They looked at one another.

'That settles it,' says Mr Quincey. 'Delicacies worthy to be set before her not available nearer than Wycombe, but must be had. There's going to be a pleasant little dinner here tonight.'

'The hussy!' says Miss Bulstrode, under her breath.

They whispered together for a moment, then they turns to me.

'Good afternoon, Mrs Meadows,' says Mr Quincey. 'You needn't say we called. He wanted to be alone, and it might vex him.'

I said I wouldn't, and I didn't. They climbed back into the motor and went off.

Before dinner I had call to go into the woodshed. I heard a scuttling as I opened the door. If I am not mistaken, Miss Dorton was hiding in the corner where we keep the coke. I didn't see any good in making a fuss, so I left her there. When I got back to the kitchen, Cook asked me if we'd got any parsley.

'You'll find a bit in the front,' I says, 'to the left of the gate,' and she went out. She came back looking scared.

'Anybody keep goats round here?' she asked me.

'Not that I know of, nearer than Ibstone Common,' I says.

'I could have sworn I saw a goat's face looking at me out of the gooseberry bushes while I was picking the parsley,' she says. 'It had a beard.'

'It's the half light,' I says. 'One can imagine anything.'

'I do hope I'm not getting nervy,' she says.

I thought I'd have another look round, and made the excuse that I wanted a pail of water. I was stooping over the well, which is just under the mulberry tree, when something fell close to me and lodged upon the bricks. It was a hairpin. I fixed the cover carefully upon the well in case of accident, and when I got in I went round myself and was careful to see that all the curtains were drawn.

Just before we three sat down to dinner again I took Cook aside.

'I shouldn't go for any stroll in the garden tonight,' I says. 'People from the village may be about, and we don't want them gossiping.' And she thanked me.

Next night they were there again. I thought I wouldn't spoil the dinner, but mention it afterwards. I saw to it again that the curtains were drawn, and slipped the catch of both the doors. And just as well that I did.

I had always heard that Mr Parable was an amusing speaker, but on previous visits had not myself noticed it. But this time he seemed ten years younger than I had ever known him before; and during dinner, while we were talking and laughing quite merry like, I had the feeling more than once that people were meandering about outside. I had just finished clearing away, and Cook was making the coffee, when there came a knock at the door.

'Who's that?' says Mr Parable. 'I am not at home to anyone.'

'I'll see,' I says. And on my way I slipped into the kitchen.

'Coffee for one, Cook,' I says, and she understood. Her cap and apron were hanging behind the door. I flung them across to her, and she caught them; and then I opened the front door.

They pushed past me without speaking, and went straight into the parlour. And they didn't waste many words on him either.

'Where is she?' asked Miss Bulstrode.

'Where's who?' says Mr Parable.

'Don't lie about it,' said Miss Bulstrode, making no effort to control herself. 'The hussy you've been dining with?'

'Do you mean Mrs Meadows?' says Mr Parable.

I thought she was going to shake him.

'Where have you hidden her?' she says.

It was at that moment Cook entered with the coffee.

If they had taken the trouble to look at her they might have had an idea. The tray was trembling in her hands, and in her haste and excitement she had put on her cap the wrong way round. But she kept control of her voice, and asked if she should bring some more coffee.

'Ah, yes! You'd all like some coffee, wouldn't you?' says Mr Parable. Miss Bulstrode did not reply, but Mr Quincey said he was cold and would like it. It was a nasty night, with a thin rain.

'Thank you, sir,' says Cook, and we went out together.

Cottages are only cottages, and if people in the parlour persist in talking loudly, people in the kitchen can't very well help overhearing.

There was a good deal of talk about 'fourteen days,' which Mr Parable said he was going to do himself, and which Miss Dorton said he mustn't, because, if he did, it would be a victory for the enemies of humanity. Mr Parable said something about 'humanity' which I didn't rightly hear, but, whatever it was, it started Miss Dorton crying; and Miss Bulstrode called Mr Parable a 'blind Samson,' who had had his hair cut by a designing minx who had been hired to do it.

It was all French to me, but Cook was drinking in every word, and when she returned from taking them in their coffee she made no bones about it, but took up her place at the door with her ear to the keyhole.

It was Mr Quincey who got them all quiet, and then he began to explain things. It seemed that if they could only find a certain gentleman and persuade him to come forward and acknowledge that he began a row, that then all should be well. Mr Quincey would be fined forty shillings, and Mr Parable's name would never appear. Failing that, Mr Parable, according to Mr Quincey, could do his fourteen days himself.

'I've told you once,' says Mr Parable, 'and I tell you again, that I don't know the man's name, and can't give it you.'

'We are not asking you to,' says Mr Quincey. 'You give us the name of your tango partner, and we'll do the rest.'

I could see Cook's face; I had got a bit interested myself, and we were both close to the door. She hardly seemed to be breathing.

'I am sorry,' says Mr Parable, speaking very deliberate like, 'but I am not going to have her name dragged into this business.'

'It wouldn't be,' says Mr Quincey. 'All we want to get out of her is the name and address of the gentleman who was so anxious to see her home.'

'Who was he?' says Miss Bulstrode. 'Her husband?'

'No,' says Mr Parable, 'he wasn't.'

'Then who was he?' says Miss Bulstrode. 'He must have been something to her—fiancé?'

'I am going to do the fourteen days myself,' says Mr Parable. 'I shall come out all the fresher after a fortnight's complete rest and change.'

Cook leaves the door with a smile on her face that made her look quite beautiful, and, taking some paper from the dresser drawer, began to write a letter.

They went on talking in the other room for another ten minutes, and then Mr Parable lets them out himself, and goes a little way with them. When he came back we could hear him walking up and down the other room.

She had written and stamped the envelope; it was lying on the table.

'"Joseph Onions Esq.,"' I says, reading the address. '"Auctioneer and House Agent, Broadway, Hammersmith." Is that the young man?'

'That is the young man,' she says, folding her letter and putting it in the envelope.

'And was he your fiancé?' I asked.

'No,' she says. 'But he will be if he does what I'm telling him to do.'

'And what about Mr Parable?' I says.

'A little joke that will amuse him later on,' she says, slipping a cloak on her shoulders. 'How once he nearly married his cook.'

'I shan't be a minute,' she says. And, with the letter in her hand, she slips out.

Mrs Meadows, we understand, has expressed indignation at our publication of this interview, she being under the impression that she was simply having a friendly gossip with a neighbour. Our representative, however, is sure he explained to Mrs Meadows that his visit was official; and, in any case, our duty to the public must be held to exonerate us from all blame in the matter.

Mr Joseph Onions, of the Broadway, Hammersmith, auctioneer and house agent, expressed himself to our representative as most surprised at the turn that events had subsequently taken. The letter that Mr Onions received from Miss Comfort Price was explicit and definite. It was to the effect that if he would call upon a certain Mr Quincey, of Harcourt Buildings, Temple, and acknowledge that it was he who began the row at the Earl's Court Exhibition on the evening of the twenty-seventh, that then the engagement between himself and Miss Price, hitherto unacknowledged by the lady, might be regarded as a fact.

Mr Onions, who describes himself as essentially a business man, decided before complying with Miss Price's request to take a few preliminary steps. As the result of judiciously conducted inquiries, first at the Vine Street police station and secondly at Twickenham, Mr Onions arrived later in the day at Mr Quincey's chambers, with, to use his own expression, all the cards in his hand. It was Mr Quincey who, professing himself unable to comply with Mr Onion's suggestion, arranged the interview with Miss Bulstrode. And it was Miss Bulstrode herself who, on condition that Mr Onions added to the undertaking the further condition that he would marry Miss Price before the end of the month, offered to make it two hundred. It was in their joint interest—Mr Onions regarding himself and Miss Price as now one—that Mr Onions suggested her making it three, using such arguments as, under the circumstances, naturally occurred to him—as, for example, the damage caused to the lady's reputation by the whole proceedings, culminating in a night spent by the lady, according to her own account, on Ham Common. That the price demanded was reasonable Mr Onions considers as proved by Miss Bulstrode's eventual acceptance of his terms. That, having got out of him all that he wanted, Mr Quincey should have 'considered it his duty' to communicate the entire details of the transaction to Miss Price, through the medium of Mr Andrews, thinking it, 'as well she should know the character of the man she proposed to marry,' Mr Onions considers a gross breach of etiquette as between gentlemen; and having regard to Miss Price's after behaviour, Mr Onions can only say that she is not the girl he took her for.

Mr Aaron Andrews, on whom our representative called, was desirous at first of not being drawn into the matter; but on our representative explaining to him that our only desire was to contradict false rumours likely to be harmful to Mr Parable's reputation, Mr Andrews saw the necessity of putting our representative in possession of the truth.

She came back on Tuesday afternoon, explained Mr Andrews, and I had a talk with her.

'It is all right, Mr Andrews,' she told me. 'They've been in communication with my young man, and Miss Bulstrode has seen the magistrate privately. The case will be dismissed with a fine of forty shillings, and Mr Quincey has arranged to keep it out of the papers.'

'Well, all's well that ends well,' I answered, 'but it might have been better, my girl, if you had mentioned that young man of yours a bit earlier.'

'I did not know it was of any importance,' she explained. 'Mr Parable told me nothing. If it hadn't been for chance, I should never have known what was happening.'

I had always liked the young woman. Mr Quincey had suggested my waiting till after Wednesday. But there seemed to me no particular object in delay.

'Are you fond of him?' I asked her.

'Yes,' she answered, 'I am fonder than—' And then she stopped herself suddenly and flared scarlet. 'Who are you talking about?' she demanded.

'This young man of yours,' I said. 'Mr—what's his name—Onions?'

'Oh, that!' she answered. 'Oh, yes; he's all right.'

'And if he wasn't?' I said, and she looked at me hard.

'I told him,' she said, 'that if he would do what I asked him to do, I'd marry him. And he seems to have done it.'

'There are ways of doing everything,' I said; and, seeing it wasn't going to break her heart, I told her just the plain facts. She listened without a word, and when I had finished she put her arms round my neck and kissed me. I am old enough to be her grandfather, but twenty years ago it might have upset me.

'I think I shall be able to save Miss Bulstrode that three hundred pounds,' she laughed, and ran upstairs and changed her things. When later I looked into the kitchen she was humming.

Mr John came up by the car, and I could see he was in one of his moods.

'Pack me some things for a walking tour,' he said. 'Don't forget the knapsack. I am going to Scotland by the eight-thirty.'

'Will you be away long?' I asked him.

'It depends upon how long it takes me,' he answered. 'When I come back I am going to be married.'

'Who is the lady?' I asked, though, of course, I knew.

'Miss Bulstrode,' he said.

'Well,' I said, 'she—'

'That will do,' he said. 'I have had all that from the three of them for the last two days. She is a Socialist, and a Suffragist, and all the rest of it, and my ideal helpmate. She is well off, and that will enable me to devote all my time to putting the world to rights without bothering about anything else. Our home will be the nursery of advanced ideas. We shall share together the joys and delights of the public platform. What more can any man want?'

'You will want your dinner early,' I said, 'if you are going by the eight-thirty. I had better tell Cook—'

He interrupted me again.

'You can tell Cook to go to the devil,' he said.

I naturally stared at him.

'She is going to marry a beastly little rotter of a rent collector that she doesn't care a damn for,' he went on.

I could not understand why he seemed so mad about it.

'I don't see, in any case, what it's got to do with you,' I said, 'but, as a matter of fact, she isn't.'

'Isn't what?' he said, stopping short and turning on me.

'Isn't going to marry him,' I answered.

'Why not?' he demanded.

'Better ask her,' I suggested.

I didn't know at the time that it was a silly thing to say, and I am not sure that I should not have said it if I had. When he is in one of his moods I always seem to get into one of mine. I have looked after Mr John ever since he was a baby, so that we do not either of us treat the other quite as perhaps we ought to.

'Tell Cook I want her,' he said.

'She is just in the middle—' I began.

'I don't care where she is,' he said. He seemed determined never to let me finish a sentence. 'Send her up here.'

She was in the kitchen by herself.

'He wants to see you at once,' I said.

'Who does?' she asked.

'Mr John,' I said.

'What's he want to see me for?' she asked.

'How do I know?' I answered.

'But you do,' she said. She always had an obstinate twist in her, and, feeling it would save time, I told her what had happened.

'Well,' I said, 'aren't you going?'

She was standing stock still staring at the pastry she was making. She turned to me, and there was a curious smile about her lips.

'Do you know what you ought to be wearing?' she said. 'Wings, and a little bow and arrow.'

She didn't even think to wipe her hands, but went straight upstairs. It was about half an hour later when the bell rang. Mr John was standing by the window.

'Is that bag ready?' he said.

'It will be,' I said.

I went out into the hall and returned with the clothes brush.

'What are you going to do?' he said.

'Perhaps you don't know it,' I said, 'but you are all over flour.'

'Cook's going with me to Scotland,' he said.

I have looked after Mr John ever since he was a boy. He was forty-two last birthday, but when I shook hands with him through the cab window I could have sworn he was twenty-five again.

The War

One of my earliest recollections is of myself seated on a shiny chair from which I had difficulty in not slipping, listening to my father and mother and a large, smiling gentleman talking about Peace. There were to be no more wars. It had all been settled at a place called Paree. The large gentleman said Paris. But my mother explained to me, afterwards, that it meant the same. My father and my mother, so I gathered, had seen a gentleman named Napoleon, and had fixed it up. The large gentleman said, with a smile, that it didn't look much like it, just at present. But my father waved his hand. Nothing could be done all at once. One prepared the ground, so to speak.

'The young men now coming forward,' said my mother, 'they will see to it.'

I remember feeling a little sad at the thought that there would be no more war—that, coming too late into the world, I had missed it. My mother sought to comfort me by talking about the heavenly warfare which was still to be had for the asking. But, in my secret heart, it seemed to me a poor substitute.

With the coming of the *Alabama* claim things looked brighter. My father, then president of the Poplar branch of the International Peace Association, shook his head over America's preposterous demands. There were limits even to England's love of Peace.

Later on, we did have a sort of a war. Nothing very satisfying: one had to make the best of it: against a King Theodore, I think, a sort of nigger. I know he made an excellent Guy Fawkes. Also he did atrocities, I remember.

At this period France was 'The Enemy'. We boys always shouted 'Froggy' whenever we saw anyone who looked like a foreigner. Crécy and Poitiers were our favourite battles. The King of Prussia, in a three-cornered hat and a bobtailed wig, swung and creaked in front of many a public house.

I was at school when France declared war against Prussia in 1870. Our poor old French master had a bad time of it. England, with the exception of a few cranks, was pro-German. But when it was all over: France laid low, and the fear of her removed: our English instinct to sympathize always with the underdog—not a bad trait in us—asserted itself; and a new Enemy had to be found.

We fixed on Russia.

Russia had designs on India. The Afghan War was her doing. I was an actor at the time. We put on a piece called *The Khyber Pass*—at Ashley's, if I remember rightly. I played a mule. It was before the Griffith Brothers introduced their famous donkey. I believe, if I had been given a free hand, I could have made the little beast amusing. But our stage manager said he didn't want any of my damned clowning. It had to be a real mule, the pet of the regiment. At the end, I stood on my hind legs, and waved the British flag. Lord Roberts patted my head, and the audience took the roof off, nearly.

I was down on my luck when the Russo-Turkish War broke out. There were hopes at first that we might be drawn into it. I came near to taking the Queen's shilling. I had slept at a dosshouse the night before, and had had no breakfast. A sergeant of Lancers stopped me in Trafalgar Square. He put his hands on my shoulders and punched my chest.

'You're not the first of your family that's been a soldier,' he said. 'You'll like it.'

It was a taking uniform: blue and silver with high hessian boots. The advantages of making soldiers look like mud had not then been discovered.

'I'm meeting a man at the Bodega,' I said. 'If he isn't there I'll come straight back.'

He was there; though I hadn't expected him. He took me with him to a coroner's inquest, and found a place for me at the reporter's table. So, instead, I became a journalist.

The music hall was the barometer of public opinion in those days. Politicians and even Cabinet Ministers would often slip in for an hour. MacDermott was our leading lion comique. One night he sang a new song: 'We don't want to fight, but by jingo if we do.' Whatever happened, the Russians should not have Con-stan-ti-no-ple, the 'no' indefinitely pro-longed. It made a furore. By the end of the week, half London was singing it. Also it added the word jingo to the English language.

Peace meetings in Hyde Park were broken up, the more fortunate speakers getting off with a ducking in the Serpentine. The Peacemonger would seem to be always with us. In peacetime we shower palm leaves upon him. In wartime we hand him over to the mob. I remember seeing Charles Bradlaugh, covered with blood and followed by a yelling crowd. He escaped into Oxford Street and his friends got him away in a cart. Gladstone had his windows broken.

And, after all, we never got so much as a look in. 'Peace with honour,' announced Disraeli; and immediately rang down the curtain. We had expected a better play from Disraeli.

To console us, there came trouble in Egypt. Lord Charles Beresford was the popular hero. We called him Charlie. The Life Guards were sent out. I remember their return. It was the first time London had seen them without their helmets and breastplates. Lean, worn-looking men on skeleton horses. The crowd were disappointed. But made up for it in the evening.

And after that there was poor General Gordon and Majuba Hill. It may have been the other way round. Some of us blamed Gladstone and the Nonconformist conscience. Others thought we were paying too much attention to cricket and football, and that God was angry with us. Greece declared war on Turkey. Poetical friends of mine went out to fight for Greece; but spent most of their time looking for the Greek army, and when they found it didn't know it, and came home again. There were fresh massacres of Armenians. I was editing a paper called *To-Day*, and expressed surprise that no healthy young Armenian had tried to remove 'Abdul the damned,' as William Watson afterwards called him. My paragraph reached him, by some means or another, and had the effect of frightening the old horror. I had not expected such luck. The Turkish Constitution used to be described as 'despotism tempered by assassination.' Under the old regime, the assassin, in Turkey, took the place of our Leader of the Opposition. Every Turkish sultan lived in nightly dread of him. I was hauled up to the Foreign Office. A nice old gentleman interviewed me.

'Do you know,' he said, 'that you have rendered yourself liable to prosecution?'

'Well, prosecute me,' I suggested. Quite a number of us were feeling mad about this thing.

He was getting irritable.

'All very well for you to talk like that,' he snapped. 'Just the very way to get it home into every corner of Europe. They can't be wanting that.'

The 'they' I gathered to be the Turkish Embassy people.

'I am sorry,' I said. 'I don't seem able to help you.'

He read to me the Act of Parliament, and we shook hands and parted. I heard no more of the matter.

It was about this time that America made war upon Spain. We, ourselves, had just had a shindy with America over some godforsaken place called Venezuela, and popular opinion was if anything pro-Spanish. The American papers were filled with pictures of Spanish atrocities, in the time of Philip II. It seemed the Spaniards had the habit of burning people alive at the stake. Could such a nation be allowed to continue in possession of Cuba?

The Fashoda incident was hardly unexpected. For some time past, France had been steadily regaining her old position of 'The Enemy'. Over the Dreyfus case it occurred to us to tell her what we thought of her, generally. In return, she mentioned one or two things she didn't like about us. There was great talk of an entente with Germany. Joe Chamberlain started the idea. The popular press, seized with a sudden enthusiasm for the study of history, discovered we were of Teutonic origin. Also it unearthed a saying of Nelson's to the effect that every Englishman should hate a Frenchman like the Devil. A society was formed for the promotion of amicable relationship between the English and the German-speaking peoples. 'Friends of Germany,' I think it was called. I remember receiving an invitation to join it, from Conan Doyle. An elderly major, in Cairo, who had dined too well, tore down the French flag, and performed upon it a new dance of his own invention. This was, I believe, the origin of the foxtrot. One of the Northcliffe papers published a *feuilleton*, picturing the next war: England— her navy defeated by French submarines—was saved, just in the nick of time, by the arrival of the German fleet.

The Boer War was not popular at first. The gold mines were so obviously at the bottom of it. Still, it was a war, even if only a sort of a war, as the late Lord Halsbury termed it. A gentleman named Perks resigned from the presidency of the Peace Society, in order to devote himself to war work. Other members followed his example. There were Boer atrocities. But they were badly done and, for a while, fell flat.

It was the Kaiser's telegram that turned the wind. I was in Germany at the time, and feeling was high against the English. We had a party one evening, at which some Dutch ladies were present—relations of De Wet, we learnt afterwards. I remember in the middle of the party, our *Dienstmädchen* suddenly appearing and shouting '*Hoch die Buren,*' and immediately bursting into tears. She explained to my wife, afterwards, that she couldn't help it—that God had prompted her. I have noticed that trouble invariably follows when God appears to be interesting himself in foreign politics.

In France it was no better. Indeed, worse. In Paris, the English were hooted in the street, and hunted out of the cafés. I got through by talking with a strong American accent that I had picked up during a lecturing tour through the States. Queen Victoria was insulted in the French Press. The *Daily Mail* came out with a leader headed '*Ne touchez pas la Reine*,' suggesting that if France did not mend her manners we should 'roll her in the mud,' take away her colonies, and give them to Germany. The Kaiser had explained away his famous telegram. It seemed he didn't really mean it. In a speech at the Vagabonds' Club, I suggested that God, for some unrevealed purpose of his own, had fashioned even Boers, and was denounced the next morning in the press for blasphemy.

At the time, there was much discussion throughout Europe as to when the twentieth century really began. The general idea was that it was going to bring us luck. France was decidedly reforming. On the other hand, Germany was 'dumping' things upon us. She was dumping her goods, not only in England, but also in other countries, where hitherto we had been in the habit of dumping ours undisturbed. After a time we got angry. There was talk of an entente with France, who wasn't dumping anything—who hadn't much to dump. The comic papers took it up. France was represented to us as a lady, young and decidedly attractive. Germany as a fat elderly gentleman, with pimples and his hair cropped close. How could a gentlemanly John Bull hesitate for a moment between them!

Russia also, it appeared, had been misunderstood. Russia wasn't half as bad as we had thought her: anyhow, she didn't dump.

And then, out of sheer cussedness as it seemed, Germany, in feverish haste, went on building ships.

Even the mildest among us agreed that Britannia could tolerate no rival on the waves. It came out that Germany was building four new cruisers. At once we demanded eight. We made a song about it.

We want eight,
And we won't wait.

It was sung at all the by-elections. The Peace parties won moral victories.

Sir Edward Grey has been accused of having 'jockeyed' us into the war— of having so committed us to France and Russia that no honourable escape was possible to us. Had the Good Samaritan himself been our Foreign

Secretary, the war would still have happened. Germany is popularly supposed to have brought us into it by going through Belgium. Had she gone round by the Cape of Good Hope, the result would have been the same. The herd instinct had taken possession of us all. It was sweeping through Europe. I was at a country tennis tournament the day we declared war on Germany. Young men and maidens, grey-moustached veterans, pale-faced curates, dear old ladies: one and all expressed relief and thankfulness. 'I was so afraid Grey would climb down at the last moment'—'It was Asquith I was doubtful of. I didn't think the old man had the grit'—'Thank God, we shan't read "Made in Germany" for a little time to come.' Such was the talk over the teacups.

It was the same whichever way you looked. Railway porters, cabmen, workmen riding home upon their bicycles, farm labourers eating their bread and cheese beside the hedge: they had the faces of men to whom good tidings had come.

For years it had been growing, this instinct that Germany was 'The Enemy'. In the beginning we were grieved. It was the first time in history she had been called upon to play the part. But that was her fault. Why couldn't she leave us alone—cease interfering with our trade, threatening our command of the sea? Quite nice people went about saying: 'We're bound to have a scrap with her. Hope it comes in my time'—'Must put her in her place. We'll get on all the better with her afterwards.' That was the idea everywhere: that war would clear the air, make things pleasanter all round, afterwards. A party, headed by Lord Roberts, clamoured for conscriptions. Another party, headed by Lord Fisher, proposed that we should seize the German fleet and drown it. Books and plays came out one on top of another warning us of the German menace. Kipling wrote, openly proclaiming Germany the Foe, first and foremost.

In Germany, I gather from German friends, similar thinking prevailed. It was England that, now secretly, now openly, was everywhere opposing a blank wall to German expansion, refusing her a place in the sun, forbidding her the seas, plotting to hem her in.

The pastures were getting used up. The herds were becoming restive.

The only contribution of any value a private citizen can make towards the elucidation of a national upheaval is to record his own sensations.

I heard of our declaration of war against Germany with cheerful satisfaction. The animal in me rejoiced. It was going to be the biggest war in history. I thanked whatever gods there be that they had given it in my time. If I had been anywhere near the age limit I should have enlisted.

I can say this with confidence because later, and long after my enthusiasm had worn off, I did manage to get work in quite a dangerous part of the front line. Men all around me were throwing up their jobs, sacrificing their careers. I felt ashamed of myself, sitting in safety at my desk, writing articles encouraging them, at so much a thousand words. Of course, not a soul dreamt the war was going to last more than a few months. Had we known, it might have been another story. But the experts had assured us on that point. Mr Wells was most emphatic. It was Mr Wells who proclaimed it a holy war. I have just been reading again those early letters of his. A Miss Cooper Willis has, a little unkindly, reprinted them. I am glad she did not do the same with contributions of my own. The newspapers had roped in most of us literary gems to write them special articles upon the war. The appalling nonsense we poured out, during those hysterical first weeks, must have made the angels weep, and all the little devils hold their sides with laughter. In justice to myself, I like to remember that I did gently ridicule the 'war to end war' stuff and nonsense. I had heard that talk in my babyhood: since when I had lived through one of the bloodiest half centuries in history. War will go down before the gradual growth of reason. The movement has not yet begun.

But I did hate German militarism. I had seen German *Offizieren* swaggering three and four abreast along the pavements, sweeping men, women and children into the gutter. (I had seen the same thing in St Petersburg. But we were not bothering about Russia, just then.) I had seen them, insolent, conceited, overbearing, in café, theatre and railway car, civilians compelled everywhere to cringe before them, and had longed to slap their faces. In Freiburg, I had seen the agony upon the faces of the young recruits, returning from forced marches under a blazing sun, their bleeding feet protruding from their boots. I had sat upon the blood-splashed bench and watched the *Mensur*—helpful, no doubt, in making the youngsters fit for 'the greatest game of all,' as Kipling calls it. I hated the stupidity, the cruelty of the thing. I thought we were going to free the German people from this juggernaut of their own creation. And then make friends with them.

At first, there was no hate of the German people. King George himself set the example. He went about the hospitals, shook hands with wounded Hans and Fritz. The captain of the *Emden* we applauded, for his gallant exploits against our own ships. Kitchener's dispatches admitted the bravery of the enemy. Jokes and courtesies were exchanged between the front trenches. Our civilians, caught by the war in Germany, were well treated. The good feeling was acknowledged, and returned.

Had the war ended with the falling of the leaves—as had been foretold by both the Kaiser and our own Bottomley—we might—who knows?—have realized that dream of a kinder and a better world. But the gods, for some purpose of their own, not yet perhaps completed, ordained otherwise. It became necessary to stimulate the common people to prolonged effort. What surer drug than hate?

The atrocity stunt was let loose.

A member of the Cabinet had suggested to me that I might go out to America to assist in English propaganda. On the ship, I fell in with an American deputation returning from Belgium. They had been sent there by the United States government to report upon the truth—or otherwise—of these stories of German frightfulness. The opinion of the deputation was that, apart from the abominations common to all warfare, nineteen-twentieths of them would have to be described as 'otherwise'.

It was these stories of German atrocities, turned out day by day from Fleet Street, that first caused me to doubt whether this really was a holy war. Against them I had raised my voice, for whatever it might be worth. If I knew and hated the German military machine, so likewise I knew, and could not bring myself to hate, the German people. I had lived among them for years. I knew them to be a homely, kind, good-humoured folk. Cruelty to animals in Germany is almost unknown. Cruelty to woman or child is rarer still. German criminal statistics compare favourably with our own. This attempt to make them out a nation of fiends seemed to me as silly as it was wicked. It was not clean fighting. Of course, I got myself into trouble with the press; while a select number of ladies and gentlemen did me the honour to send me threatening letters.

The deputation published their report in America. But it was never allowed to reach England.

America, so far as I could judge, appeared to be mildly pro-French and equally anti-English. Our blockade was causing indignation. In every speech I made in America, the only thing sure of sympathetic response was my reference to the 'just and lasting' peace that was to follow. I had been told to make a point of that. A popular cartoon, exhibited in Broadway, pictured the nations of Europe as a yelling mob of mud-bespattered urchins engaged in a meaningless scrimmage; while America, a placid motherly soul, was getting ready a hot bath and bandages. President Wilson, in an interview I had with him, conveyed to me the same idea: that America was saving herself to come in at the end as peacemaker. At a dinner to which I was invited, I met an important group of German business men and bankers. They assured me that Germany had already grasped the fact that she had bitten off more than she could chew, to use their own expression, and would welcome a peace conference, say at Washington. I took their message back with me, but the mere word 'conference' seemed to strike terror into every British heart.

It was in the autumn of 1916 that I 'got out,' as the saying was. I had been trying to get there for some time. Of course my age, fifty-five, shut all the usual doors against me. I could have joined a company of 'veterans' for home defence, and have guarded the Crystal Palace, or helped to man the Thames Embankment; but I wanted to see the real thing. I had offered myself as an entertainer to the YMCA. I was a capable raconteur and had manufactured, or appropriated, a number of good stories. The YMCA had tried me on home hospitals and camps and had approved me. But the War Office would not give its permission. The military gentleman I saw was brief. So far as his information went, half the British army were making notes for future books. If I merely wanted to be useful, he undertook to find me a job in the Army Clothing Department, close by in Pimlico. I suppose my motives for wanting to go out were of the usual mixed order. I honestly thought I would be doing sound work, helping the Tommies to forget their troubles; and I was not thinking of writing a book. But I confess that curiosity was also driving me. It is human nature to jump out of bed and run a mile merely to see a house on fire. Here was the biggest thing in history taking place within earshot. At Greenwich, when the wind was in the right direction, one could hear the guns. Likewise masculine craving for adventure. Quite conceivably, one might get oneself mixed up with excursions and alarms: come back a hero. Anyhow, it would be a relief to get away, if only for a time, from the hinterland heroes with their shrieking and their cursing. The soldiers would be gentlemen.

I had all but abandoned hope, when one day, outside a photographer's shop in Bond Street, I met an old friend of mine, dressed up in the uniform of a major-general, as I took it to be at first sight.

You could have knocked me down with a feather. I knew him to be over fifty, if a day. The last time I had seen him, about three weeks before, had been in his office. He was a solicitor. I had gone to him about some tea leaves my wife had been saving up. She was afraid of getting into trouble for hoarding.

He shook hands haughtily. 'Sorry I can't stop,' he said. 'Am sailing from Southampton tonight. Must look in at the French Legation.'

'One moment,' I persisted. 'Can't you take me out with you, as your aide-de-camp? I don't mind what I do. I'm good at cleaning buttons—'

He waved me aside. 'Impossible,' he said. 'Joffre would—'

And then, looking at my crestfallen face, the soldier in him melted. The kindly stout solicitor emerged. Taking out a notebook, he wrote upon a page. Then tore it out and gave it me.

'You can tell them I sent you,' he said. 'Ta-ta.' He dived into a waiting taxi. The crowd had respectfully made way for him.

It was an address in Knightsbridge that he had given me. I saw a courteous gentleman named Illingworth, who explained things to me. The idea had originated with a French lady, La Comtesse de la Panousse, wife of the military attaché to the French Embassy in London. The French army was less encumbered than our own with hidebound regulations. Age, so long as it was not accompanied by decrepitude, was no drawback to the driving of a motor ambulance. I passed the necessary tests for driving and repairs, and signed on. Thus I became a French soldier: at two and a half sous a day (paid monthly; my wife still has the money). The French Legation obtained for me my passport. At the British War Office I could snap my fingers. Passing it, on my last day in London, I did so: and was spoken to severely by the constable on duty.

Upon our uniform, I must congratulate La Comtesse de la Panousse. It was, I understand, her own creation: a russet khaki relieved by dark blue facings, with a sword belt and ornamental buttons. It came expensive. Of course, we paid for it ourselves. But I am sure that none of us begrudged the money. The French army did not quite know what to make of us. Young recruits assumed us, in the dusk, to be field marshals. One day, in company with poor Hutchinson, the dramatist, who died a few months after he got back to England, I walked through the gateway of the Citadelle at Verdun, saluted in awed silence by both sentries.

I sailed from Southampton in company with Springs-Rice, brother to our ambassador at Washington, and our chef de section, D.L. Oliver, who was returning from leave in England. We took out with us three new cars, given by the British Farmers' Association. The ship was full of soldiers. As we stepped on deck, we were handed life collars, with instructions to blow them out and tie them round our necks. It gave us an Elizabethan touch. One man with a pointed beard, an officer of Engineers, we called Shakespeare. Except for his legs, he looked like Shakespeare. But lying down in them was impossible. Under cover of darkness, we most of us disobeyed orders, and hid them under our greatcoats. Passing down the Channel was like walking down Regent Street on a Jubilee night. The place was blazing with lights. Our transport was accompanied by a couple of torpedo destroyers. They raced along beside us like a pair of porpoises. Every now and then they disappeared, the waves sweeping over them. About twelve o'clock the alarm was given that a German submarine had succeeded in getting through. We returned full speed to Southampton dock, and remained there for the next twenty-four hours. On the following night, we were ordered forward again; and reached Havre early in the morning. The cross-country roads in France are designed upon the principle of the maze at Hampton Court. Every now and then you come back to the same village. To find your way through them, the best plan is to disregard the signposts and trust to prayer. Oliver had been there before but, even with that, we lost our way a dozen times. The first night we reached Caudebec, a delightful medieval town hardly changed by so much as a stone from the days of Joan of Arc, when Warwick held it for the English. If it hadn't been for the war, I would have stopped there for a day or two. As it was, Springs-Rice and myself were eager to get to the front. Oliver, who had had about a year of it, was in less of a hurry. At Vitry, some hundred miles the other side of Paris, we entered 'the zone of the Grand Armies,' and saw the first signs of war. Soon we were running through villages that were little more than rubbish heaps. The Quakers were already there. But for the Quakers, I doubt if Christianity would have survived this particular war. All the other denominations threw it up. Where the church had been destroyed the Friends had cleared out a barn, roofed it, and found benches and a home-made altar—generally, a few boards on trestles, with a white cloth and some bunches of flowers. Against the shattered walls they had improvised shelters and rebuilt the hearthstone. Old men and women, sitting in the sun, smiled at us. The children ran after us cheering. The dogs barked. Towards evening I got lost. I was the last of the three. Over the winding country roads—or rather cart tracks—it was difficult to keep in touch. I knew we had to get to Bar-le-Duc. But it was dark when I struck a little town called Revigny. I decided to stop there for the night. Half of it was in ruins. It was crowded with troops, and trains kept coming in discharging thousands more. The *poilus* were lying in the streets, wrapped in their blankets, with their knapsacks for a pillow. The one miserable hotel was reserved for officers. My uniform obtained me admission. The *salle-à-manger* was crammed to suffocation: so the landlady put me a chair in the kitchen. The cockroaches were having a bad time. They fell into the soups and stews, and no one took the trouble to rescue them. I secured some cold ham and a bottle of wine; and slept in my own ambulance on one of the stretchers. I pushed on at dawn; and just outside Bar-le-Duc met Oliver, who had been telephoning everywhere, inquiring for a lost

Englishman. I might have been court-martialled, but the good fellow let me off with a reprimand; and later on I learnt the trick of never losing sight of the car in front of you. It is not as easy as it sounds. At Bar-le-Duc we learnt our destination. Our unit, Convoi 10, had been moved to Rarécourt, a village near Clermont in the Argonne, twenty miles from Verdun. We reached there that same evening.

We were a company of about twenty Britishers, including colonials. Amongst us were youngsters who had failed to pass their medical examination, and one or two officers who had been invalided out of the army. But the majority were, like myself, men above military age. Other English sections, similar to our own, were scattered up and down the line. The Americans, at that time, had an ambulance service of their own: some of them were with the Germans. A French officer was technically in command; but the chief of each section was an Englishman, chosen for his knowledge of French. It was a difficult position. He was responsible for orders being carried out and, at the same time, was expected to make things as easy as possible for elderly gentlemen unused to discipline: a few of whom did not always remember the difference between modern warfare and a Piccadilly club. Oliver was a marvel of tact and patience. We drew the ordinary army rations. Meat and vegetables were good and plentiful. For the rest, we had a mess fund, and foraged for ourselves. Marketing was good fun. It meant excursions to Ste Menehould or Bar-le-Duc, where one could get a bath, and eat off a clean tablecloth. For messroom, we had a long tent in the middle of a field. In fine weather it was cool and airy. At other times, the wind swept through it, and the rain leaked in, churning the floor into mud. We sat down to *la soupe*, as our dinner was called, in our greatcoats with the collars turned up. For sleeping, we were billeted about the village. With three others I shared a granary. We spread our sleeping sacks upon stretchers supported on trestles, and built ourselves washing stands and dressing tables out of packing cases that we purchased from the proprietress of the *épicerie* at a franc a piece. Later, I found a more luxurious lodging in the house of an old peasant and his wife. They never took their clothes off. The old man would kick off his shoes, hang up his coat, and disappear with a grunt into a hole in the wall. His wife would undo hidden laces and buttons and give herself a shake, put her shoes by the stove, blow out the lamp, and roll into another hole opposite. There was a house near the church with a bench outside, underneath a vine. It commanded a pretty view, and of an evening, when off duty, I would sit there and smoke. The old lady was talkative. She boasted to me, one evening, that three officers, a colonel and two majors, had often sat upon that very bench the year before and been quite friendly. That was when the Germans had occupied the village. I gathered the villagers had made the best of them. 'They had much money,' added Madame.

Firing was our difficulty. It's an ill wind that blows nobody good. The news that a shelled village had been finally abandoned by its inhabitants flew like wildfire. It was a question of who could get there first, and drag out the timbers from the shattered houses. Green wood was no good: though, up in the dugouts, it was the only thing to be had. They say there is no smoke without fire. It is not true. You can have a dugout so full of smoke that you have to light a match to find the fire. If it's only French matches you have, it may take a boxful. It was our primus stoves that saved us. Each man's primus was his vestal fire. We kept them burning day and night: cooked by them, dried our clothes, and thawed our feet before going to bed. Mud was our curse. The rain never ceased. We lived in mud. Our section worked the Argonne forest. Our *point de secours*, where we waited, was some hundred yards or so behind the front trenches. The wounded, after having passed through the field dressing station, were brought to us on stretchers; or came limping to us, twisting their faces as they walked. So long as we were within call we could wander at our will, creep to where the barbed wire ended, and look out upon the mud beyond. Black, silent, still, like some petrified river piercing the forest: floating on it, here and there, white bones, a man's boot (the sole uppermost), a horse's head (the eyes missing). Among the trees the other side, the stone shelters where the German sentries watched.

The second night I was on duty, I heard a curious whistling just above my head. I thought it some night bird, and looked up. It came again, and I moved a few steps to get a better view. Suddenly something butted me in the stomach and knocked me down; and the next moment I heard a loud noise, and a little horse, tethered to a tree some few yards off, leapt up into the air and dropped down dead. It was Monsieur le Médecin, a chemist from Peronne, who had bowled me over, and was dragging me down the steps into his dugout. I didn't hang about another time, when I heard that whistling in the trees.

There must have been some means of communication between the men themselves on either side. During the two hours, every afternoon, when the little tramway was kept busy hauling up food, both French and German batteries were silent. When the last barrel of flour, the last sack of potatoes, had been rolled in safety down the steps of the field kitchen, the firing would break out again. When a German mine exploded, the Frenchmen who ought to have been killed were invariably a quarter of a mile away sawing wood. One takes it that the German peasant lads possessed like gift of intuition, telling them when it would be good for their health's sake to take walking exercise.

A pity the common soldiers could not have been left to make the peace. There might have been no need for Leagues of Nations. I remember one midday coming upon two soldiers, sitting on a log. One was a French *poilu* and the other his German prisoner. They were sharing the Frenchman's lunch. The conqueror's gun lay on the ground, between them.

It was the night call that we dreaded. We had to drive without lights: through the dense forest, up and down steep, narrow ways with sudden turns and hairpin bends—one had to trust to memory: and down below, in the valley, where the white mists into which one strained one's eyes till it felt as if they were dropping out of their sockets. We had to hasten all we dared, the lives of men behind us depending upon time. Besides, we might be wanted for another journey. We often were. There ought at times to have been a moon, according to the almanac: but to that land of ceaseless rain she rarely came. It was nerve-racking work. The only thing to do was not to think about it till the moment came. It is the advice that is given, I understand, to men waiting to be hanged. One takes off one's boots, and tunic, blows out the candle and turns in. A rat drops from somewhere onto the table, becomes immovable. By the light of the smouldering logs, we look at one another. One tries to remember whether one really did put everything eatable back into the tin. Even then they work the covers off, somehow—clever little devils. Well, if he does, he does. Perhaps he will be satisfied with the candle. Ambulance Driver Nine turns his head to the wall. Suddenly he is up again. A footstep is stumbling along the wooden gangway. It is coming nearer. He holds his breath. The gods be praised, it passes. With a sigh of relief he lies down again, and closes his eyes.

The next moment—or so it seems to him—a light is flashing in his eyes. A bearded, blue-coated figure is standing over him. Ambulance to start immediately! (*'Ambulance faut partir!'*) The bearded figure, under its blue iron helmet, kindly lights the candle (rat having providentially found something more tasty) and departs. Ambulance Driver Nine struggles half unconsciously into his clothes and follows up the steps. Pierre, the *aide*, is already grinding away at the starting handle, and becoming exhausted. One brushes him aside and takes one's turn, and with the twentieth swing—or thereabouts—the car answers with a sudden roar, as of some great drowsy animal awakened from its slumbers; and Pierre, who has been cursing her with all the oaths of Gascony, pats her on the bonnet and is almost amo-rous. A shadowy group emerges apparently from the ground. Two stretchers and three *assis* is the tale. The stretchers are hoisted up and fitted swiftly into their hangings. The three *assis* mount slowly and shuffle painfully into their places. Rifles and knapsacks are piled up beside them, and the doors are clanged to. Another 'case' is to be picked up on the way—at Champ Cambon. You take the first road on the left, after passing the ruins of the Ferme de Forêt, and the camp is just beyond the level crossing. It seems you cannot miss it. And Ambulance Driver Nine climbs into his seat.

Through the forest, he keeps his eyes upon the strip of sky above his head. Always he must be in the exact centre of that narrow strip of sky. And it will wobble. Pierre sits on the footboard, his eyes glued to the road. '*Gauche, gauche,*' he cries suddenly. Driver Number Nine pulls the wheel to the left. '*A droit,*' shrieks Pierre. Which the devil does he mean? And what has become of the sky? Where's the damned thing gone to? The deep ditch that he knows to be on either side of the road seems to be calling to him like some muddy Lorelei. Suddenly the sky reappears. It seems to have come from behind him. He breathes once more.

'*Arrêtez,*' cries Pierre, a little later. He has detected a vague, shapeless mass that might be the ruins of a farm. He descends. One hears his footsteps, squelching through the mud. He returns triumphant. It is a farm. Things seem to be shaping well. Now, all they have to do is to look out for a road on the left. Thy find a road on the left—or hope they have. The descent appears to be steep. The car begins to jump and jolt. '*Doucement, camarade—douce-ment!*' comes an agonised cry from within. Pierre opens the little window and explains that it cannot be helped. It is a *mauvaise route*: and there is silence. The route becomes more and more *mauvaise*. Is it a road, or are they lost? Every minute the car seems as if it were about to stand on its head. Ambulance Driver Nine recalls grim stories of the messroom: of nights spent beside a mud-locked car, listening to groans and whispered prayers: of cars overturned, their load of dying men mingled in a ghastly heap of writhing limbs, from which the bandages have come undone. In spite of the damp chill night, a cold sweat breaks out all over him. Heedless of Pierre's remonstrances, he switches on his electric torch and flashes it downwards. Yes, it is a road of sorts, chiefly of shellholes, apparently. The car crashes in and out of them. If the axles do not break, by some miracle. Pierre gives a whoop of joy as the car straightens herself out. They have reached the level, and the next moment they bump over the crossing, and hear the welcome voice of a sentry.

The *blessé* is brought out. He has been unconscious for two hours. Driver Nine had best make speed. The mist that fills the valley grows whiter and whiter. It is like a damp sheet, wrapped round his head. Shadows move towards him, and vanish; but whether they were men or trees or houses he cannot tell. Suddenly he jams on his brakes and starts up. It is clear enough this time—a huge munition wagon, drawn by a team of giant horses. They are rearing and plunging all round him.

But no sound comes from them! Pierre has sprung to the ground and is shouting. Where is their driver?

The whole thing has vanished. They listen. All is silence. Pierre climbs up again and they break into a loud laugh.

But why did Pierre see it, too!

They crawl along on bottom gear. There comes a low crashing sound. Even the torch is useless, a yard in front of them. They find by feeling that they are up against a door. Fortunately the back wheels are still on the road, so that they can right themselves. But it seems useless going on. Suddenly, Pierre dives beneath the car and emerges, puffing a cigarette. He dances with delight at his own cleverness. He holds the lighted cigarette behind his back and walks jauntily forward, feeling the road with his feet. Ambulance Driver Nine drives on, following the tiny spark. Every now and then, the invisible Pierre puffs the cigarette, covered by his hand, and it reappears with a brighter glow. After a time the mist rises; and Pierre bursts into song and remounts. A mile or so farther on they reach the barrier, beyond which lamps are permitted, but decide not to light up. Their eyes are in training now, and had better not be indulged; it will spoil them for the journey back. They are both singing different tunes when they arrive at the base hospital, twenty kilometres behind the lines.

'Have any trouble?' asks a fellow-driver from another section, who has just discharged his load and is drawing on his gloves.

'The mist was a bit trying,' answers Driver Nine. 'We had to come round by Champ Cambon.'

'Nasty bit of road, that, down the hill,' agrees the other. 'So long!'

From Rarecourt we were moved to Verdun. It was in ruins then. From some of the houses merely the front wall had fallen, leaving the rooms intact, just as one sees them in an open doll's house: two chairs drawn close together near the hearth, the crucifix upon the wall, a child's toy upon the floor. In a shop were two canaries in their cage, starved to death, a little heap of feathers that fell to pieces when I touched them. In a restaurant, the soup still stood upon the table, the wine half finished in the glasses.

The Citadelle was still occupied: an underground city of galleries and tunnels, streets of dormitories, messrooms, a concert hall, stores, hospitals and kitchens. Here and there, one came across groups of German prisoners removing the debris, tidying up generally. There must have been great shortage of wool in Germany, at that time. It was a bitter winter, yet the most of them had no underclothing but a thin cotton shirt. One could see their naked bodies through the holes. A company of French Engineers were quartered in the cathedral. The altar served them for a kitchen table. The town was strangely peaceful, though all around the fighting still continued. Our unit, Section 10, had been there the winter before, during the battle, and had had a strenuous time. During the actual fighting, Hague Conventions and Geneva Regulations get themselves mislaid. The guns were eating up ammunition faster than the little tramways could supply them, and the ambulances did not always go up empty. Doubtless the German Red Cross drivers had likewise their blind eye. It is not the soldiers who shout about these things. The Germans were accused of dropping shells onto the hospitals. So they did. How could they help it? The ammunition park was one side of the railway head and the hospital the other. It was the most convenient place for both. Those who talk about war being a game ought to be made to go out and play it. They'd find their little book of rules of not much use. Once we were ordered to take a company of staff officers on a tour of inspection. That did seem going a bit too far. Springs-Rice bluntly refused: but not all of us had his courage.

From rain the weather had turned to frost. Often the thermometer would register forty degrees below zero. The Frenchmen said it was '*pas chaud.*' A Frenchman is always so polite. It might hurt the weather's feelings, telling it bluntly that it was damn cold. He hints to it that it isn't exactly warm, and leaves the rest to its conscience. Starting the cars was horses' work. We wrapped our engines up in rugs at night and kept a lamp burning under the bonnet. One man made a habit of using a blowpipe to warm his cylinders, and the rest of us gave him a wide berth. The birds lost the use of their wings. They lay huddled up wherever there was shelter from the wind. Some of the soldiers took them scraps of food, but others caught and cooked them. It wasn't worth the trouble: there was nothing on them.

One day, in a wood, I chanced upon a hospital for animals. It was a curious sight. The convalescents were lying about in the sun, many of them still wearing bandages. One very little donkey was wearing the Croix de Guerre. His driver had been killed and he had gone on by himself, with a broken leg, and had brought his load of letters and parcels safely up to the trenches. The transport drivers were kind to their beasts; and many of the soldiers had their little dog that marched with them and shared their rations. But they used to pour petrol over the rats, when they caught them, and set fire to them. 'He ate my sausage,' a bright-eyed little *poilu* once answered me. He regarded it as an act of plain justice. Some of the officers had made gardens in front of their dugouts; and the little cemeteries, dotted here and there about the forest, were still bright with flowers when I first saw them. A major I used to visit had furnished his dugout with pieces of genuine Louis Quatorze: they had been lying about the fields when he had got there. We used to drink coffee out of eggshell china cups. In the villages farther back, life went on much as usual. Except when a bombardment was actually in progress, the peasants still worked in the fields, the women gossiped and the children played about the fountain. Bombardment or no bombardment, mass was celebrated daily in the church—or what was left of it. A few soldiers made the congregation, with here and there a woman in black. But on Sundays came the farmers with their wives and daughters in fine clothes and the soldiers—on weekdays not always spick and span—had brushed their uniform and polished up their buttons.

But within the barrier, which ran some ten kilometres behind the front, one never saw a woman or a child. Female nurses came no nearer than the hospitals at the base. It was a dull existence, after the first excitement had worn off. We worried chiefly about our food. The parcel from home was the great event of the week. Often, it had been opened. We had to thank God for what was left. Out of every three boxes of cigarettes that my wife sent me, I reckon I got one. The French cigarettes, that one bought at the canteens, were ten per cent poison and the rest dirt. The pain would go out of a wounded soldier's face when you showed him an English cigarette. Rum was our only tipple, and the amount that each man could purchase was limited. It was kind to us, and warmed our feet. The Paris papers arrived in the evening—when they did arrive. They told us how gay and confident we were. For news, we preferred reading the daily bulletin, posted up each morning outside headquarters: it told the truth, whether pleasant or unpleasant. We got used to the booming of the guns. At the distance of a few miles the sound was not unmusical. Up in the dugouts, we were close to our own batteries. They were cleverly hidden. I remember once sitting down upon a log to read. It was a pretty spot, underneath a bank that sheltered one from the wind. Suddenly something happened. I thought, at first, my head had come off. I was lying on the ground, and became aware of a pair of eyes looking at me through a hole in the bank. I had been sitting outside a battery of seventy-fives. The boyish young officer invited me inside. He thought I'd be more comfortable. Round Verdun, they barked incessantly and got upon one's nerves. Sometimes the order would be given for 'all out' on both sides, and then the effect was distinctly terrifying. But one had to creep out and look. The entire horizon would be ablaze with flashlights, stars and rockets, signalling orders to the batteries. Towards dawn the tumult would die down; and one could go to bed. One had no brain for any but the very lightest literature. Small books printed on soft paper, the leaves of which could be torn out easily, were the most popular. We played a sort of bridge and counted the days to our leave. The general opinion among the French was that the English had started the war to capture German trade, and had dragged France into it. There was no persuading them of their mistake.

It had been a trying winter, and my age had been against me. At the end of it, I was not much more good for the work. I came back cured of any sneaking regard I may have ever had for war. The illustrations in the newspapers, depicting all the fun of the trenches, had lost for me their interest. Compared with modern soldiering, a street scavenger's job is an exhilarating occupation, a rat-catcher's work more in keeping with the instincts of a gentleman. I joined a little company who, in defiance of the press and of the mob, were making an appeal for a reasonable peace. We made speeches in Essex Hall and in the provinces. Among others on our platform, I recall Lord Parmoor, Lord Buckmaster, the Earl of Beauchamp, Ramsay MacDonald, Dean Inge, Zangwill, the Snowdens, Drinkwater, and E.D. Morel the great-hearted. We had one supporter in the press, *Common Sense*, edited by F.W. Hirst, who right through the war kept his flag flying with tact and good humour. Later, Lord Lansdowne came to our aid. Lord Northcliffe, who died not long afterwards of a lingering brain disease, suggested he must be suffering from senile decay. Whether we did any good, beyond satisfying our own consciences, I cannot say.

The war ended in 1918. From 1919 to 1924 there was every prospect of France's regaining her old position as 'The Enemy'. Reading the French papers, one gathered that nothing would please France better. At the present moment (1925) a growing party would seem to be in favour of substituting Russia. It may be that the gods have other plans. The white are not the only herds. The one thing certain is that mankind remains a race of low intelligence and evil instincts.